SCOTT
Numt

CW01497423

Alan Spence's

*Its Colours
They Are Fine*

and

Way To Go

John Burns

Association for Scottish Literary Studies 2010

Published by
Association for Scottish Literary Studies
Department of Scottish Literature
7 University Gardens
University of Glasgow
Glasgow G12 8QH
www.asls.org.uk

ASLS is a registered charity no. SC006535

First published 2010

© John Burns

A CIP catalogue for this title
is available from the British Library

ISBN 978-1-906841-02-7

The Association for Scottish Literary Studies
acknowledges the support of Creative Scotland
towards the publication of this book.

Printed by Bell and Bain Ltd., Glasgow

CONTENTS

SCOTNOTES

Study guides to major Scottish writers and literary texts

Produced by the Education Committee
of the Association for Scottish Literary Studies

THE ASSOCIATION FOR SCOTTISH LITERARY STUDIES aims to promote the study, teaching and writing of Scottish literature, and to further the study of the languages of Scotland.

To these ends, the ASLS publishes works of Scottish literature; literary criticism and in-depth reviews of Scottish books in *Scottish Literary Review*; short articles, features and news in *ScotLit*; and scholarly studies of language in *Scottish Language*. It also publishes *New Writing Scotland*, an annual anthology of new poetry, drama and short fiction, in Scots, English and Gaelic. ASLS has also prepared a range of teaching materials covering Scottish language and literature for use in schools.

All the above publications are available as a single 'package', in return for an annual subscription. Enquiries should be sent to:

ASLS
Department of Scottish Literature
7 University Gardens
University of Glasgow
Glasgow G12 8QH

Tel/fax +44 (0)141 330 5309
e-mail **office@asls.org.uk**
or visit our website at **www.asls.org.uk**

The page references in this study guide are to the following editions:

Its Colours They Are Fine, London: Phoenix, 1996 (P)

Its Colours They Are Fine, Glasgow: Collins, 1977 (C)

Way to Go, London: Phoenix House, 1998 (hardback), 1999 (paperback)

1. ALAN SPENCE: HIS LIFE AND WORK

Alan Spence was born in Govan, Glasgow, in 1948. Although he now divides his time between Edinburgh where he lives, and Aberdeen University where he is Professor of Creative Writing, Glasgow is an all-pervasive presence in his voice and in his writing.

He began writing seriously when in Sixth Year at Alan Glen's Secondary School and, encouraged by his English teacher Paddy Inglis, produced some poetry for the school magazine. The magazine won *The Scotsman*'s School Magazine Competition in 1966. Later, at Glasgow University where he studied Law before changing to English, he came under the influence of Tom McGrath who was the focus for a group of writers which included Tom Leonard, Alasdair Gray and Liz Lochhead. Contact with such a group encouraged Spence's interest in writing and helped him to develop a confidence in his own voice. It also led him to do a stint at the Edinburgh Festival Fringe in 1968 where a reading of his story 'Silver in the Lamplight' so caught the imagination of editor Bob Tait that he published it in his influential magazine *Scottish International*. Many of the stories in *Its Colours They Are Fine* (1977) were first published in that magazine.

Another important encounter around this time was Spence's meeting with his spiritual teacher Sri Chinmoy which happened on 2nd December, 1970: 'Three days before my twenty-third birthday, I can date it precisely', he told Alan Taylor of *The Sunday Herald* on 16th March, 2003 – more than thirty years later. Currently Spence and his wife jointly run the Sri Chinmoy Centre in Edinburgh and teach meditation.

Spence's writing is both funny and moving. He evokes the lives of his predominantly working class characters with insight and tenderness, showing how ordinary people actually live their lives in difficult circumstances. In highlighting the inadequacies of our society there is a strong political undertow to his writing, but even more central to his work is the idea of the spiritual quest. He has identified two main reasons why this is so: the shock of his mother's early death when he was eleven years old; and the fact that in the 1960s and early

1970s an interest in Eastern philosophy was 'in the air'. Losing his mother affected him deeply and forced him to start 'looking for answers', to try to make sense of a world that can hold such suffering. After an early commitment to Christianity which is described in the story 'Christian Endeavour' in *Stone Garden* he picked up on the general mood of the times and read many of the available books on what Alan Watts called Eastern 'ways of liberation'. These ways of liberation give us practical methods to help see through the illusions that surround us to the reality that lies behind all the illusions – to the way things are, and not the way we would like them to be. Meeting Sri Chinmoy gave Alan Spence a way to move his quest from a theoretical to a practical level through the discipline of meditation. Already a published writer before this meeting, it confirmed him in his vocation, and gave a deeper validity to what he was trying to do in his writing.

Sri Chinmoy's teaching has been central to Spence's life and work since that first meeting. It has given him the stamina and insight to develop his writing as well as a strong impulse to help others develop their own writing. His commitment to creative writing has been clear in the many Writer in Residence posts he has held and in particular in the energy he has brought to the post in Aberdeen where his role in creating and developing the Word Festival in that city has been crucial.

Spence is an accomplished writer in several genres. He is a poet, dramatist, novelist and short story writer. He has written for television and for radio. He has written for workers in their factories and for children in schools. His work is always accessible, and always full of depth and insight.

Spence lists several early influences including Dylan Thomas, especially his stories because 'they were like nothing I'd read before. They seemed to be about ordinary, everyday life, and yet written with this heightened poetic vividness'. Other influences he has acknowledged are Joyce, Chekhov, Allan Sillitoe and Neil Gunn. From these writers he absorbed different aspects that inform his own work. From Thomas there was the magical sound of the words while from Sillitoe there was the 'grit' of realism and the primacy of the local voice.

From Chekhov an interest in the oblique and fugitive, the way a chance moment can reveal so much about a character's life. Joyce, of course, is the master of the epiphany, able to illuminate our experience by focusing on moments of insight into the numinous. Gunn, too, with his interest in Zen Buddhism and his 'atoms of delight', showed that ordinary life for ordinary people is filled with the possibility of suddenly realising just how extraordinary the ordinary world is.

The vision that informs Spence's writing then is a positive one. This is partly through temperament, and partly through training (in meditation). It is also a vision that Spence has developed over many years in the face of personal suffering and a difficult adolescence following the death of his mother and his father's decline after his wife's death. Spence's positive vision is no glib evasion of reality: it is born out of a deep personal engagement with human suffering that results in writing that is filled with insight and compassion.

2. ITS COLOURS THEY ARE FINE

Introduction
Published in 1977 *Its Colours They Are Fine* was immediately recognised as a classic. Allan Massie in *The Scotsman* (27 August, 1977) praised the sensitivity of Spence's prose, his objectivity and lack of sentimentality and went on to say:

> In this book, Mr Spence has achieved a rarity; a piece of writing as convincing as a Cezanne or Matisse. It really has the quality of great painting. What Mr Spence will do next is a matter of the utmost importance for Scottish literature. And one shouldn't be narrowly parochial about it: for the future of whatever is written in any variety of the English language. He's in that league.

The book's title refers to the song 'The Sash My Father Wore', a song that immediately draws attention to the religious bigotry that still divides much of Scotland today. One of Spence's achievements in the book is to use a potentially negative title and show through the action of his stories that despite the bigotry, the poverty, the social deprivation, life is a marvellous and colourful thing: its colours they are indeed fine.

For the characters in Spence's stories living conditions were cramped, often consisting of just 'a room and kitchen' off a communal tenement stair with limited access to a shared toilet. Flats were overcrowded and often damp which adversely affected the health of people who were already poor and undernourished. As a major industrial centre Glasgow, in the nineteen forties and nineteen fifties, was often smoky and dark. Communities were split along religious lines. For many to be a Protestant or a Roman Catholic was to pledge allegiance to one side or the other which automatically meant that the other side was wrong or 'bad'. It is a way of thinking that has caused untold hurt and damage in our society, and a way of thinking that Spence has always questioned, while still being able to write sensitively about those who hold such views. In *Scottish Writers Talking 2* Spence describes Govan 'circa 1965–6' as 'one of the bleakest places on the planet'[1]. Like many ordinary

4

people living in that place, Spence's parents did their best to live decent lives and worked hard to give him opportunities that had been denied to them, especially through education. His novel *Way To Go* is movingly dedicated to the memory of his parents in recognition of this.

The thirteen stories of *Its Colours They Are Fine* are all set in Glasgow and explore the lives of ordinary people living in that city. The model for this was probably James Joyce's *Dubliners* (1914), his collection of stories looking at the 'paralysis' of the lives of its characters, all told in a style of 'scrupulous meanness'. Joyce's work is echoed and alluded to throughout *Its Colours They Are Fine,* from the accuracy of Spence's Glasgow dialogue to the way the action of individual stories recalls the action of stories in *Dubliners.* 'The Ferry' for instance reminds us of 'An Encounter' in its picture of the young boys in the wasteland. 'Araby', in particular, might be seen as especially important in the way that Joyce shows a young narrator being awakened to the loss and sadness that is inherent in all human life, a theme that can be traced through all of Spence's writing and which is closely linked to the early loss of his mother and to his subsequent study of Hinduism and Buddhism.

Joyce's example showed that it is possible to write about 'ordinary' experience in such a way as to highlight its extraordinariness – the intensity of each individual's experience being given value and dignity. In *Writers in Scotland* Spence describes the moment he realised that he could write about his own world:

> I had grown up in Glasgow, Govan, in fact, which wasn't the most beautiful part of the planet, and kind of looking around for things to write about ... I remember looking out of the window one time, and feeling a wee bit cheated in comparison with folk like Dylan Thomas in terms of what they had to write about, and it was like one of those wee moments of revelation where I thought, no, this is what you've got to write about: [...] the tenements and the middens and the wine drinkers and scabby dugs and the housing schemes.[2]

The chronology of this is uncertain, but such an insight is both central to the teachings of Sri Chinmoy, and something that Spence feels almost viscerally as part of his own nature. He goes on to point out that 'I don't sit down consciously to write a story which will make a particular religious or social point'.[3] Sri Chinmoy's teachings seemed to confirm insights that Spence had already had.

In these thirteen stories Spence creates a picture of modern Glasgow that is immediately recognisable in its gritty, grimy reality but which also holds the possibility of transcendence. He does this by not shirking the uncomfortable reality of his characters' physical existence: he suggests strongly that their perceived poverty of imagination is often caused by the poverty and social deprivation that is the reality of their lives.

The stories of Part One of *Its Colours They Are Fine* look at the world of the children. Like Joyce, like Neil Gunn, Spence is very good at re-creating the sharp intensity of a child's awareness of the world. As he said to Fiona Norris:

> Everything's absolutely total when you're a kid ... I think that when folk are remembering their own childhood they're remembering that clarity [of perception] and that intensity and that vividness that's there when you're a kid. And also it's an attempt ... to understand how you've become what you are as an adult.[4]

In *Highland River* (1937), Gunn had evoked that sharp intensity of perception of the world seen in great detail from a particular perspective, from a particular *height*, even, so that the child's world is to a large extent an awareness and love of small things that adults often miss. It is a form of perception that delights in the physical intimacy of the world and it is a way of being in the world that many of us lose as we 'grow up'. Both Joyce, in *A Portrait of the Artist As A young Man* (1916), and Gunn in *Morning Tide* (1930) and *Highland River* (1937) used a simple style and simple language to suggest the peculiar intensity of this way of experiencing the world.

Stories from Part One of *Its Colours They Are Fine*

'Tinsel'

In 'Tinsel', Spence shows his mastery of this style from the beginning when he takes us into the mind of a sensitive young boy who is waiting for his mother to finish doing her washing at the communal washhouse or 'steamie':

> The swing doors of the steamie had windows in them but even when he stood on tiptoe he couldn't reach up to see out [...] So he had to be content to peer out through the narrow slit between the doors, pressing his forehead against the brass handplate [...] He could smell the wood and paint of the door and the clean bleachy smell from the washhouse. His eye began to sting from the draught [...] When the doors had stopped swinging [after a woman came through] and settled back into place he noticed that the brass plate was covered with finger marks. He wanted to see it smooth and shiny so he breathed up on it, clouding it with his breath, and rubbed it with his sleeve. (P:3; C:11)

It is a long quotation because as it appears in the book every word adds to our sense of the character and involves us in his world. Not only is he observant and intensely aware of his physical surroundings using almost all of his senses to 'place' himself, but Spence also suggests that this is partly due to his anxiety at being even temporarily separated from his mother. He is old enough to observe his world and make sense of it, but he is young enough to be uncertain of his own place in it: his sense of personal identity is still fragile enough that he needs to confirm it through his relationship with his mother. In a story that is about family this is singularly apt.

The story goes on to describe the boy's family preparing for Christmas. We are introduced to the boy's mother and father and we see their love and care for each other and for their son. Both suffer from chronic illnesses possibly connected to their poverty and are concerned for each other's health. They are also careful not to alarm their son. Their living conditions are poor but typical for many working class families in

Glasgow at that time. They live in a room and kitchen and can only afford to heat one or the other, and they share a toilet on the landing with other families. Spence portrays them as an ordinary family trying to make the best of their lot.

He describes the boy's excitement at helping his parents sort out the Christmas decorations. To go with last year's decorations his father has bought something special: an 'UN-TARNISHABLE SILVER GARLAND'. The boy is fascinated by it and his parents together explain the meaning of the new words: untarnishable means 'it canny get wasted. It always steys nice and shiny'. (P:12; C:19) The boy's father has to go out to buy more tacks and while he is away he and his mother manage to put the decorations up with sellotape:

> When they heard his father's key in the door his mother shooshed and put out the light. They were going to surprise him. He came in and fumbled for the switch. They were laughing and when he saw the decorations he smiled but he looked bewildered and a bit sad. (P:13; C:20)

In a brief access of vision the boy suddenly understands the reason for his father's sadness:

> Then they understood. He was sad because they'd done it all without him. Because they hadn't waited. (P:13; C:20)

This moment of vision, an example of what Zen Buddhists call *kensho*, is for the boy the beginning of an awareness of the sadness at the heart of life, a first intimation of mortality. His father passes the moment off lightly but when the boy looks into the reflection in the kitchen window:

> He imagined it was another room jutting out beyond the window, out into the dark. He could see the furniture, the curtain across the bed, his mother and father, the decorations and through it all, vaguely, the buildings, the night. And hung there, shimmering in that room he could never enter, the tinsel garland that would never ever tarnish. (P:13; C: 21)

At first glance this could appear rather depressing, but it is at heart a creative vision ('He *imagined* ...'), an active engagement with the world that involves not only the awareness of mortality and loss, but also the imperative of the quest: the human need always to seek wisdom and enlightenment. What Spence has done here is to take an ordinary moment in the lives of very ordinary people and give it huge significance. That significance will be expanded and given even more authenticity and authority through his succeeding books, but in *Its Colours They Are Fine* it is given particular significance in the final story 'Blue' which describes the beginning of this family's disintegration with the death of the boy's mother.

'The Ferry'

The quest is a central organising motif in 'The Ferry' which takes the young boy now named Aleck through a series of adventures with his pal Joe. Their quest is for adventure, but the real quest is for enlightenment and freedom as signalled by Spence in the opening paragraph when he describes the boys' cane arrow seeming to fly free of the tenements that 'enclosed' them, before 'turning back to complete its arc and fall to land with a jar that staved and shuddered its whole length on the hardpacked dirt and brick of the back court' (P:30; C:36). The arc of the arrow's flight is mirrored in the arc of the boys' attempt to break free of their life in poverty in Govan.

Spence is very good at showing us again that intensity of involvement, the 'seriousness', with which the boys engage in their games. The liveliness and accuracy of his dialogue too is instrumental in involving the reader in the world the boys inhabit:

> 'Heh Aleck, comin wull no bother gawn back tae school? Wull jist rin away an dog it forever.'
> 'That wid be brilliant!' said Aleck. 'Wherr could we go?'
> Joe held up his arrow.
> 'We could go tae America an live wi REAL Indians. Ah've goat an auntie in Canada.'

'Ach thur's nae real Indians left,' said Aleck. 'They aw get
pit oot'n daft wee reservations.'
    'How aboot India then?' said Joe. 'Or Africa? We could
live in a tree hoose.'
    'Pick bananas 'n oranges,' said Aleck.
    'Hunt animals.' (P:31; C:37)

Innocently ignorant of the reality of the world beyond their
immediate locality the boys try their best to make sense of it.
Like most children they have picked up attitudes and their
sense of who they are from those around them. Both boys are
imaginative, but as the story progresses we see that Aleck
has the confidence to engage more imaginatively with the
new world being revealed to him through education. It is not,
however, an easy path.
    When one of their arrows lands near some pigeon-fanciers
Aleck thinks:

Watching the pigeons was a mystery with its secrets, its
initiates, a language of its own. (P: 33-34; C:39)

He sees them as a secret brotherhood with their own ritu-
als and secrets all centred round the worship of the birds but
his reverie about the softness and gracefulness of the birds is
quickly shattered when he tries to retrieve the arrow:

One of the men picked up the arrow. He looked straight at
Aleck and snapped the arrow in two. He was grinning.
    'Aw … izzat no a shame … ah've went an broke it!'
    The others laughed and he threw the pieces aside.
    'Get tae buggery wi yer bows 'n arras or ah'll snap yer
fuckin neck!'
    Aleck ran and scrambled back across the wall. (P:34;
C:40)

The apparently thoughtless violence of this is striking. In
an attempt to explore their world the boys are met by a cal-
lous display of adult meanness of spirit. For Aleck, trying to
find a place in the world, it is a small but significant defeat

that crushes his spirit just that little bit more. To be a child in this world is difficult, as growing up is constantly undermined by the very people who are supposed to serve as role models.

Picking themselves up from this defeat the boys decide on another adventure 'efter tea'. They will cross the river to Partick and explore the far side of the river. The sense of difference, of *otherness*, is marked and has been reinforced by their education:

> Miss Riddie had told them about Partick and Govan growing side by side [...] She had said they were like reflections, Partick and Govan, with the river like a mirror in between. (P:38; C:43)

The boys enjoy the trip on the ferry but having 'charged' up the steps in their excitement they suddenly feel less certain of themselves:

> The grey buildings looked the same, but they were not their own. They felt lost and threatened [...] At the corner opposite, a group of men loafing. Boys their own age, playing, looking towards them [...]
> 'D'you know anywherr tae go? asked Aleck.
> 'Naw. No really,' said Joe.
> 'D'ye fancy jist gawn back?'
> 'Comin?'
> 'Right, c'mon!' (P:38; C:43–4)

They realise that they are out of their depth in this new place despite its closeness to home. Reaching the other shore is not an easy transition to make. Again the dialogue is masterly. Neither boy wishes to admit his discomfiture to the other so the laconic utterances allow them to save face without giving too much away. It is a completely believable story of an incident in the lives of two wee boys, but 'reaching the other shore' is a powerful metaphor for growing up, and a common Buddhist term for reaching a state of enlightenment.

Unwilling to admit defeat and in a final act of youthful male bravado they decide just to ride the ferry back and forward over the river but the ferry pilot puts an end to their adventure by putting them off on the Partick side so that they have a long miserable walk home via another ferry further downriver. Their response is to swear helplessly at the ferry as it nears Govan without them. This is the graceless, violent language the pigeon-fanciers had directed at them earlier. It shows how patterns of behaviour are learned and repeated, and it highlights how people are trapped by them. For Buddhists this world of thoughtless habits is the world of illusion they call *samsara*. It is the world we live in; a world from which we must escape if we are to be enlightened. Yet, paradoxically, Spence shows how Aleck's swearing gives way to a more thoughtful frame of mind which suggests that perhaps he might be able to find a way to freedom from his poverty-stricken environment. The story ends with the boys climbing *upwards* to begin their journey, the awareness of their own vulnerability the beginning, for Aleck at least, of a more thoughtful approach to life and what it means to live in this fragile world.

Stories from Part Two of *Its Colours They Are Fine*

The stories in Part One of *Its Colours They Are Fine* show a boy becoming aware of his place in the world and learning its boundaries. In Part Two Spence goes on to explore the lives of the adults who live within those boundaries.

'Its Colours They Are Fine'

The story 'Its Colours They Are Fine' follows Aleck's uncle Billy through the day of the Orange Walk from leaving the house resplendent in his regalia – his sash, gloves and cuffs – to his dishevelled and drunken journey home late that night after a day of reasserting once more his loyalty to a certain set of beliefs and prejudices. The story presents these prejudices without any overt judgment, but it seems clear that Spence sees this way of life, these attitudes as destructive, injurious to the spirit of the people. The story ends with

Billy, his drunken mind full of jumbled scraps of the day's conversations, hurling his whisky bottle into the air 'into the terrible darkness of it all'. (P:93; C: 94)

'Brilliant'

'Brilliant' looks at the lives of Shuggie and Eddie, two of Aleck's schoolfriends who have left school and gone into work as labourers while Aleck stayed on. In many ways this story could be seen as one of the inspirations for Spence's novel *The Magic Flute* as the differences between the boys' attitudes and their fates is central. Shuggie and Eddie enjoy their new-found status as workers, and are quick to mock Aleck when they see him in his school uniform, carrying the flute he plays in the school orchestra. The gulf between them is vast. Seeing the flute they can imagine nothing more than Aleck learning to play 'The Sash My Father Wore' and see him as weak:

> 'Fucksake but!' said Eddie. 'E'll still be at school when e's whit ... eighteen. Ah mean imagine that! Some wee shite ae a teacher giein ye the belt for talkin!' (P:100; C:101)

For them education is threatening: either the system gave up on them or they gave up on the system. Those who succeed in that system are either 'posh' or weak. Both are terms of abuse. Shuggie, however, does realise that Aleck's education will give him advantages in life: 'E'll come oot wi a good joab an that. Nae fuckin overtime fur him.' (P:100; C:101) Despite his newfound freedom and money, Shuggie already seems to realise there is something missing from his life although he does not know what it is. He is already contemplating joining the army to escape the boredom and pointlessness of his life in Govan. He has recognised that there is more to life than making a bit of money and having a laugh with his mates; that a life driven by short-term desires is really no life at all.

The story ends bleakly when Shuggie and Eddie go to a local dance, and we see their inability to move beyond the security of the world they know. At first this is seen in the way they find it difficult to interact with the girls they so desper-

ately want to dance with. It is a scene familiar to most people
of Spence's generation: the vast bare space of the dance-floor,
the echoing of the vocals and electric guitars, the girls dancing in groups in the coloured light in the middle of the floor,
the boys hanging around uncertain on the edge of the dance-
floor. A rite of passage. Shuggie and Eddie like many young
men find genuine interaction with the girls difficult and on
this occasion impossible:

> Shuggie noticed a small blonde girl standing by herself. He
> pushed over towards her and asked her to dance.
> 'Ah'm arready wae some'dy,' she said.
> He turned away. He saw two girls dancing together. He
> stepped in between them.
> 'D'ye wanty dance wae me?' he asked one of them, his
> back to the other.
> 'Naw,' she said, shaking her head.
> 'We don't wanty get split up,' said her friend [...]
> 'Never mind Shug,' said Eddie. 'Thur no worth it. Fuck
> them all!' (P:108; C:108)

There is a bleak black humour in this. As a courtship ritual
it is rather blunt and lacking in dignity. It is certainly lacking in romance and imagination. 'D'ye wanty dance wae me?'
seems an inadequate way to invite someone to spend the rest
of their life with you. Shuggie's tragedy, however, is that he
knows deep inside that they are worth it, that love is one
of the things missing from his life. His tragedy is deepened
by the fact that his education and his background have not
given him ways to express the emotions that he feels:

> Something about the songs always got to Shuggie. He had
> a head full of them. He only had to hear the opening bar
> and he'd be filling in the backing, playing every instrument,
> adding every voice. Sweet soul music. It lit something in
> him. It was something he wanted to spill out. He wanted
> to flail his arms and sing and laugh, sharing it. But he just
> stood, watching, bobbing his head, tapping his foot, looking
> now at the girls, dancing [...] (P:107; C:107)

He cannot share his feelings, his joy, does not know how to and, therefore, he cannot enter the dance, that traditional image of life itself. Like Aleck and Joe in 'The Ferry' the young men here seem to be unable to escape their environment. In the earlier story Aleck seems to have the inner resources to learn from that defeat and move on, perhaps eventually to find a way through. Here, however, Shuggie's embarrassment and frustration can only lead to the kind of senseless violence that is all too common in modern Scotland. As they lie in wait for the two boys who are with the girls they 'fancied' Shuggie carefully feels in his pocket his steel comb with the long pointed handle and Spence ends with the boys uttering their individual opinion on their night out:

> 'Mental!' he said.
> 'Brilliant!' said Rab. (P:109; C:109)

The reader can decide for himself which it is.

'Greensleeves'

These characters in 'The Ferry' and 'Brilliant' are trapped in their lives, feel that they are locked *out* somehow from the real life that goes on around them. The old woman who narrates 'Greensleeves' locks herself *in* for the night as if to reinforce her sense of entrapment in her lonely isolated life in a flat in a tower block. A thoughtful, observant woman, she is now a displaced person, her old house 'over in Ibrox' torn down in Glasgow's re-development. Despite the wonderful view from her flat ('Sometimes she was amazed at how much there was to see' (P:165; C:161)) her life has become a lonely wait for death. The story is a moving meditation on the way elderly people are treated in our society.

'The Rain Dance'

'The Rain Dance' is a story about a wedding. It explores the lives of the young couple, Brian and Kathleen, and Kathleen's parents Tommy and Mary Brady. It is a funny and a moving account of how the wedding will change all of their lives. It is also a piece of social history in the way that it documents

many of the traditional customs of working class weddings
in Scotland in the mid twentieth century, from the parading
of the bride-to-be through the town by her workmates, to the
'scramble' where loose change is thrown for children to pick
up, and the family get-together and sing-song. Throughout,
Spence's descriptions and his use of Scots in his dialogue to de-
lineate his larger than usual cast of characters is impressive.

Despite the celebratory nature of the opening where Kathleen is paraded noisily through the housing scheme by her
friends to be kissed by the men they meet and to let the community know that tomorrow she will be married, that her
status in the community will be changed, there are those
who refuse to join in that mood of celebration. Spence pic-
tures them as 'tightlipped and knowing'. (P:110; C:110)

> 'Tommy Brady's lassie.'
>   'Gettin merried at Martha Street themorra.'
>   'Merried oantae a Proddie tae.'
>   Passing silent judgement on this double heresy. (P:110;
> C:110)

These are the nay-sayers, whose greetin faces Burns sati-
rised two hundred years ago as 'the unco-guid' but whose
baleful influence is still with us. The girls, in their joy, are
bigger than such small-minded attitudes. They have too
much life in them which spills out in laughter and ribaldry.
They wish Kathleen well and their happy laughter will accompany her into her new life.

So that bride and groom will not see each other the night
before the wedding, while Kathleen is making her rounds,
Brian has been taken for a drink by her father. The two men
get on well and Tommy obviously approves of Brian. Kathleen's mother also likes Brian but feels keenly the weight of
disapproval part of her community feels towards the wedding. She has been made to feel even worse by the attitude
of her priest:

> Mary liked Brian well enough but she was troubled about
> the wedding. She remembered that bit in the missal about

> not marrying outside the church [...] So she was worried for
> Kathleen. Father Boyle had put the fear in her about the
> wedding not being blessed. (P:113; C:113)

A decent woman, she does not have the confidence to trust
her own perceptions of the situation and feels she must defer
to the dictats of her church.

In this same section she muses on the way her life has
changed:

> Three years now Peter [Kathleen's brother] had been gone.
> And now it was Kathleen. One more day. The house would
> be strange without her. Just herself and Tommy. And Kath-
> leen and Brian would begin it all again. (P:113; C:113)

This is slipped in quite naturally by Spence and it is fully
in keeping with Mary's character at this point in her life, but
it gives expression to a thought that is central to Spence's vision: our individual identity is part of a larger whole. Mary's
perception of the *pattern* of human lives, the sense she has
that Brian and Kathleen are just like her and Tommy is part
of this. There is, too, a kind of sadness in her realisation that
it is their time now, that that time in her own life has passed.
She does, of course, now have the chance of opening up a new
phase of her life with Tommy. It is a bittersweet moment of
real insight.

The wedding goes well and the family party afterwards is
lively and good-natured with friends and relatives singing,
eating and drinking to share in the young couple's happi-
ness and mark their changed status. This section of the story
(P:125–130; C:124–130) is very lively with Spence catching
the humour and fun and sadness of it all very well. Just
as Brian and Kathleen are leaving, however, Father Boyle
turns up to 'have a word' with Tommy and Mary, apparently
unaware that the wedding is that day. His mealy-mouthed
apology for his intrusion is interrupted by Tommy, a bit the
worse for wear, bursting into the room wearing the native
American headdress he had brought home from his holiday
in Canada:

'Ah ya bastard!' Tommy was struggling with the door and
the handle had come away. The door thudded twice under
his boot then there was a final crash as it swung open and
he came stumbling into the room. 'Wahoo!' he shouted,
brandishing the doorknob. The head-dress was perched on
his head, tilted forward so that the fur covered his brow.

'I think I'll just be going,' said Father Boyle, but Tommy
came over and grabbed him by the arm.

'Hello therr Father Boyle,' he said. 'Wull ye huv a wee
half tae drink ma daughter's health?'

'I really must be going,' said the priest.

'Ach c'mon,' said Tommy. 'Melt yer auld stone face fur
wance in yer life!' (P:131; C:129)

Drunk, dressed as a Red Indian in his own living room,
Tommy cuts a ridiculous figure but his love for his daughter and his sense of justice shine through as he berates the
priest for his miserable and judgmental attitude to the lives
of the people in his care.

Having got rid of the priest, Tommy, in his guise as Medi-
cine Man or healer to the tribe, brings proceedings to a close
by performing a spectacular 'Rain Dance' for everyone there
in his house to exorcise the memory of the miserable presence of the priest.

The story ends quietly with a brief glimpse of Kathleen
and Brian beginning their new life together. And despite the
parallels with the life of Tommy and Mary Brady, this young
couple are setting out on a new life. Kathleen might make
tea just like her mother, but she and Brian are setting out
through life along a very different path:

> She took a joss-stick from the packet and lit it, blowing out
> the flame and watching it smoulder and glow. She placed it
> in the brass holder on the mantelpiece, watched the smoke
> curl and rise past the wooden image of Siva that Brian had
> bought at the Barrows, Siva with his four arms, his fire and
> his drum, dancing in a circle of flame. (P:132; C:130)

Like her mother she too looks out of the window and becomes quietly thoughtful. The rhythms of her thought though are less agitated than those of her mother, less defensive and more accepting of the world she sees. As she watches the streetlights going on she thinks kindly on the people of her city:

> She thought of them going on all over Glasgow, a linked network of lights, strung across the city, and everywhere people coming home. (P:132; C: 131)

Like many young people in the 1960s, like Alan Spence himself, Brian and Kathleen are setting out on a 'journey to the East', starting to explore Buddhism and Hinduism, the philosophies of spiritual liberation. The modesty of their involvement (the wooden Siva was bought at the Barrows) and the fact that it does not exclude their families who follow traditional Western ways of thinking, suggest that this is a genuine involvement with these philosophies and not some trendy eccentricity based on fashion and arrogant elitism.

Like the wee boy in 'Tinsel', like most of the characters we have encountered in this collection, Brian and Kathleen are on a quest, an attempt to see beyond the surface, and to live in a way that does not demean human beings but allows them to live in their world with dignity.

It is perhaps important to point out here that, despite criticism of Christianity in his work, Spence is not in any way *against* Christianity. In many stories he goes out of his way to highlight parts of the Christian message. We have seen the family Christmas in 'Tinsel', and in 'Sheaves' he simultaneously satirises the minister's glib and insincere sermonising and reawakens for his readers the beauty and the truth of Christ's parables:

> 'And no matter what happens to you, even if the dirt of the world seems to have settled on you and made you forget what you really are, deep inside you are still his golden sheaves. And no matter how drab and grey and horrible our lives and this place may sometimes seem, remember that this is only the surface. And even the muck of hundreds of

years cannot hide that other meaning which is behind all
things. The meaning that we are here to celebrate. That
God is Love and Christ is Life.' (P: 25–26; C:33)

'The Palace'

'The Palace' is also about the quest for dignity. It tells the
story of an older man who has fallen on hard times and whose
life is a struggle against despair. Out of work, his wife dead,
forced to live in cheap, shared accommodation he begins to
feel that his life is unreal. Like Mary Brady in 'Rain Dance',
he senses something of the impermanence of life:

> Sometimes things that had happened thirty or forty years
> ago were just as clear, just as real to him as anything going
> on now. He was always remembering; things were forever
> repeating themselves [...] He had grown up, married, be-
> come a father. His wife had died, his son had moved away.
> It all seemed like a dream. (P:135; C:133)

The transitory nature of life is also suggested in his
thoughts of his neighbours:

> Some of his neighbours he had never even seen. Sometimes
> he wondered about all the different people who had lived
> here. (P:136; C:134)

He thinks of the

> [...] rows of names on every door, some typewritten, some
> carefully inked, others roughly scribbled and each name
> with its own bell [...] Living here he knew was only a tran-
> sition. (P:136–7; C:134)

He does not just mean living in this house. He means that
living at all is a transitory experience. Like everything else
it will pass. The insight has come with age, that breaking
through of memory into a present where he feels cast adrift,
with no real status in his society. He is old, widowed, un-
employed and, therefore, 'invisible' in a society that thrives

on youth, sex, work and the material wealth that work can bring. Cast aside from this society his life is dreary and drab. The business of his days is to rescue a little dignity from a world that does not care about him any more.

He suffers the humiliation of having to 'sign on' at the labour exchange, wanders round Paddy's Market in search of cheap second-hand clothes, and then goes for a cheap lunch of a bacon roll and a bowl of soup at the Iona Community House. He likes the peace and quiet there and thinks that this atmosphere has something to do with it being connected to a chapel and having links to Iona. He is 'revived' by this and 'brought back to life'. When he leaves he does not feel like going back so soon to his dingy flat so decides to take refuge in the Kibble Palace – where 'it was always summer'. (P:147; C:144)

The Kibble Palace is a famous landmark. It is the glass house of Glasgow's Botanic Gardens, and a favourite haunt of its citizens. It is warm and the old man amuses himself by imagining that, as he wanders through the different sections each housing plants from different countries, he is travelling round the globe:

> It was pleasing to think that his leisurely dawdle round the Gardens would take him through four continents. (P:147; C:144)

Again he senses that the solid world he inhabits is not as solid as he had once thought:

> Passing inside he felt the warmth, the gentle humidity of the atmosphere; condensation, wetness of leaves. He breathed it in. The smell of it was green. He walked round the pond and along the passageway, through South Africa to Australia. It was a whole different world from the cold and grey outside. Sounds seemed accentuated, the crunch of his footsteps on the red ash of the path, the steady drip and spray of water from hosepipes and sprinklers, the song and chatter of tiny birds. The green was ease to the eye, creepers and tree ferns reaching up on either side, dark

luxuriant growth; it breathed a rich fragrance, vegetation,
the damp of the earth. In imagination he could be deep in
some tropical rainforest. (P:147: C:144)

Something of the peace he had felt at the Iona Community
House is still apparent here. The slow, careful rhythms of his
thought, the close attention to his heightened senses, com-
municate something of this feeling to the reader. It is a way
of seeing that is close to the heightened awareness of meditation. Not only was he 'revived' and 'brought back to life', but
in 'going for refuge' to the Palace he is engaging in one of the
most basic of Buddhist practices. To take refuge is to begin
to lose our self-importance and recognise that our sense of
our own individuality depends very much on other factors
beyond our control. It is summed up in the verse:

> I take refuge in the Buddha [the enlightened one]
> I take refuge in the Dharma [the truth, the way things ac-
> tually are]
> I take refuge in the Sangha [the community of seekers]

In this meditative frame of mind he is joined by the rather
shabby old man he had seen in the queue at the labour exchange earlier. They pass the time talking about their lives
and spend an enjoyable time sharing bad jokes and puns
with each other. It feels as if this is the longest conversation
the man has had for some time so he is glad of the company,
though he is rather wary of the old man's reaching into his
carrier bag for a bottle of wine and imagines him to be a 'dos-
ser', the kind of person to be avoided at all costs because he
is not respectable. Although happy to talk to him, he doesn't
want to slide into the netherworld of drunks and down-and-
outs. (Perhaps the reader should bear in mind the use of
wine in Holy Communion, as well as the idea of 'wine' being a
catalyst for spiritual insight in various other traditions.)
Gradually, however, he relaxes and joins him in a drink.
He reveals that he was originally from Campbeltown, like
Spence's own father, and that he still remembers it with affection. He tells the old man:

'Ah'm always rememberin things, even fae when ah wis
wee. An whit's funny is, a lot a the time it's jist daft things
that come back tae ye. Things that don't matter.' (P:154;
C:151)

Again that sense of life as a kind of dream where 'reality' is
fluid and ever-shifting. The old man, however, tells him:

That's wher yer wrong, see, cos it ALL matters. Every wee
thing [...] Course, at the same time, none ae it matters a
damn!' (P: 154; C:151)

They have a good laugh at the truth and the absurdity of
this, then the old man goes on to talk quite openly and naturally about a moment of vision that came to him when he
visited Iona.

'God,' said the old man. 'Whit a place that is.' Again he was
far away, and his voice was more quiet as he went on, feeling
for words. 'It's no like ... how kin ah explain it? It's nothin
ah could describe tae ye, y'know. Ah mean ah could tell ye
all about the place, the abbey an the ruins an the sea an
... everythin! But even if ah could describe every last wee
thing on that island, ah still wouldnae be able tae say it.
It's jist a feelin. Ther's jist this incredible peace [...] when
ah went ah wis in a bad state, cos ah'd jist lost ma wife ye
see. But as soon as ah got there ah felt this peace ah'm tel-
lin ye about. An then ther wis one evenin ... ah'd been out
for a walk an ah wis comin back down tae the abbey. An ah
stopped, an looked about me, an it wis jist getting dark, an
ther wis jist the stillness an this fine fine rain soakin intae
me, but it didnae matter, an nothing else mattered, an ther
wis jist this feelin a bein out maself ... an it wis like ah
wasn't even feelin it, there wis jist the feelin itself ... an it
wis like ther wis no time, an ah wis part a everythin that
had ever been ... an ah KNEW! (P:157; C:153–4)

Hearing the old man struggle to articulate his moment
of vision, his experience of *kensho*, causes him to have his

own momentary awakening. The movement and colour and rhythm of the fish in the pond help to create the conditions for this to happen:

> Standing at the pond, he looked down into the water, watching the fish swim slowly round, the shapes they traced, gliding, darting, the rhythm of their movement a perfect flow. Reflected in the water was the glass domed roof, a circle of sky at the bottom of the pond, the frame of the dome a radial pattern, broken by the rippling fish, the rocks, the trailing plants. (P:158; C:155)

This strangely calming image can be read as a vision of his own mind, the movement and rhythms of the fish being like the movement of his thoughts. The reflection of the circle of the dome in the water (which anticipates Spence's story 'Milan Cathedral At The Bottom Of The Sea') is a traditional symbol of wholeness, and the spokes coming out from the centre of the circle suggest the age-old symbol of psychic integration, the *mandala*.

What he finds in his own mind is a memory of his wife:

> Lying with his wife on their wedding-night, first night in their own home. Because it was wartime, furniture was scarce and they hadn't a proper bed, just a mattress in the middle of the floor. The air-raid sirens had been whining, but they were staying where they were [...] Here at least they could have a little time together. By the side of the makeshift bed they had lit a small candle [...] and in its flickering light he had lain awake half the night [...] hearing the bombs drop somewhere else, safe in her arms [...] (P:159; C:155)

The wedding night and the intimacy recall the young couple in 'Rain Dance'. The lighted candle calls to mind the joss-stick Kathleen had lit as part of the ritual of appreciation of their new life. Beginning married life during a wartime bombing raid had given him a sharper sense of the importance of their relationship. The awareness of how fragile and precarious human life can be makes him value it all the more.

A final vision comes to him, a memory of his house in Campbeltown when he was four or five years old. The swirling movement of the fish reminds him of the design on the carpet where he had played:

> The carpet had been old and frayed but the patterns had still been clear. Out of the shapes, he had made a whole world, of flowers and faces, stars and leaves, all merging into each other [...] He remembered [...] the familiar enclosing warmth of the house around him [...] safe. He remembered the feeling; centred, contained, whole [...] Every evening at the same time [his mother] would look up at the clock, and tell him his father would be on his way. And he would jump up and run outside to watch for him. And there he would be coming slowly up the steep cobbled street. And his father would wave, and he would go pounding down the hill, running to meet him in a surge of simple joy, and his father would lift him on to his shoulder and carry him home. (P:159–60; C:155–156)

Rhythmically here Spence catches the young boy's thought process through the simple sentence structures, the repeated use of 'and' building up the excitement until the final relief and resolution of coming 'home'. The Eastern idea of being centred, whole, is simply but effectively tied to the boy's love of home, the sense of his own family together in this place.

Spence's achievement here is to make us feel that such moments of vision arise naturally out of his characters' lives. There is no straining after significance. The moments are left to work on our own minds. Their naturalness makes us look at our own experience more closely, makes us realise that such moments happen all the time. There is also a slight ambiguity, however, as we are reminded that the man has been drinking although not to excess and probably not enough to affect his judgement. His head is 'clear' although the wine has left a 'sour' taste. Spence leaves us to decide whether these visions are positive or pointless.

Stories from Part Three of *Its Colours They Are Fine*

In Part Three of *Its Colours They Are Fine* Spence makes the
spiritual dimension more obvious. 'Changes' and 'Auld Lang
Syne' make explicit mention of Buddhism and Hinduism to
a much greater extent than anything we have encountered
in the book already, while 'Blue' interestingly explores a moment of insight within a Christian framework.

'Changes'

The un-named narrator of 'Changes' and 'Auld Lang Syne'
shares many similarities with Aleck, the young boy of Part One,
with Brian in 'The Rain Dance', and with Alan Spence himself.
He is also typical of many young people who grew up in the
1960s. He is educated and intelligent but has turned away from
the traditional route to success as laid out in the west: stick in
at school, go to university and get a good job which pays well:
'Twenty years of schoolin' and they put you on the day shift', as
Bob Dylan sings in 'Subterranean Homesick Blues'.

The narrator here is looking for something more in his life,
although he seems uncertain of just what this might be. At
the moment he is living a rather rootless and aimless life
and has a job working in a hospital which cares for mental
patients. In the story we meet him on a trip to London where
he has gone to stay with two old friends, Doug and Jenny. He
finds out that other old friends have moved on, have separated. Ritchie has become involved in the shadowy, violent
world of paramilitarism in Ireland while Mag has fallen foul
of drugs and was last heard of in prison. The narrator muses
on how, as they grow older, friends often drift apart, their
lives more 'fragmented'. In a line that foreshadows Spence's
novel *The Magic Flute*, Jenny says: 'It's crazy [...] the different roads we wind up takin.' (P:179; C:174)

The second half of the story describes his journey back to
Glasgow, interspersed with disturbing memories of his work
at the hospital. 'Getting back' indeed is a major theme in the
story. In the London flat when he is trying to make up his
mind just when to set off he consults the *I Ching*, the Chinese
book of divination and wisdom whose glossy black cover was

a fixture in many student flats of the 1960s and 1970s, and is delighted to read a very positive statement which convinces him that the omens are good. This feeling is strengthened when he opens his copy of R.H. Blyth's *Haiku* at the page which features the jingle on the Glasgow city coat of arms:

> This is the bell that never rang
> This is the fish that never swam
> This is the tree that never grew
> This is the bird that never flew

These things happening at the same time cause a feeling of revelation, an epiphany, the term Joyce used to define those little moments of insight that come to us all. It is, in fact, the Christian Feast of the Epiphany as Jenny suddenly realises, the twelfth day of Christmas:

> 'Time to take down the cards an things,' she said.
>   Doug got up and cleared them away. And just in that moment, I seemed to feel all the beautiful sadness of our little lives, the fullness and the transitoriness of it all.
>   Epiphany. Taking down the Christmas cards. The bare mantelpiece. (P:184; C:178–9)

That last paragraph is almost a regular haiku of 5–7–5 syllables. Like most true moments of insight it emerges unbidden out of an ordinary experience. That is why it affects the narrator so deeply. As the Quakers say, it 'speaks to his condition'. His condition is one of alienation from the world he lives in; nothing dramatic, just a feeling of unease and dissatisfaction with his life, of nothing really being worthwhile. Essentially, though, it is the 'condition' of many apparently normal people in our society.

The 'getting back' then of the story is about getting back to some kind of spiritual equilibrium. As he attempts to keep warm by the side of the motorway, dancing and singing to himself, he suddenly sees the absurdity of it all. His being there in the cold empty blackness of the night could be seen as an image of Buddhism's Great Void:

> And yet in the very heart of this emptiness came a fullness,
> a closeness to all things. The familiarity of everything.
> Friendly, the night sky. A faint humour in my old rucksack
> slumped on the grass verge. There, just so. The moment
> itself, in all its bareness and clarity.
>
> And there suddenly seemed something comic in my being
> there at all [...] So many people on so many journeys [...] I
> would get back. I knew that. (P:186; C:181)

The feeling does not last and later, as he stands, chilled to
the bone, beside the motorway in the dark, he attempts to
understand his isolation by trying to read by the faint light
from the road signs the book that Doug had given him. The
book outlines the Four Noble Truths of Buddhism. The first
Noble Truth, that all life is suffering, makes him think of the
hospital. It is not a happy thought.

When he does arrive back in Glasgow the auspicious return he had hoped for does not happen. Instead he is mugged
on the street, becomes the victim of the kind of drink-fuelled
senseless violence that is all too common in modern Scotland. The city's coat of arms painted on the side of a bus
seems to mock him. There is, however, one bright moment
for him, when he finds in his rucksack some fruit that Doug
and Jenny had given him:

> Four hundred miles from my friends, the apples they gave
> me for the journey. (P:195; C:189)

Such simple acts of kindness are important to Spence and
occur often in his work. These acts balance or cancel out the
numerous acts of verbal or physical abuse that occur to his
characters.

In the last section of the story the changes of the title become more important, so that the words of the *I Ching* that
he had read in London begin to resonate more fully:

> Change is the law of nature and society; when decay has
> reached its climax a recovery must take place. (P:182;
> C:177)

The 'changes' then of the title are the ceaseless interaction of yin and yang, that Buddhists and Taoists see as the Tao, the way of things. One of the meanings of Tao, of course, is 'way' in the sense of a path or a journey. The journey back for our narrator is not just a physical one; it is a spiritual journey as well. Part of that journey is the realisation that working in the hospital is not right for him: it is not his way, so he must find something else:

> The place was numbing me. I would distance myself from it while I was actually there. I would cope. Then on my way home I'd feel like crying. Grey and depressed, I'd feel physically sick. (P:199; C:192–3)

He comes to the liberating decision to leave, recognising that in his depressed frame of mind he is no use to the patients, that he might actually be a hindrance to them. He realises that he cannot help others find wholeness if he is not whole himself:

> I could talk about wholeness. But what I had to do was find it in myself. The job might be just one more necessary experience. But I knew now I couldn't go back. I was doing no good, to myself or anybody else. (P;199; C:193)

It is no use knowing the theory. You have to feel it in your bones.

His last moment of insight comes when he 'stopped in at the Art Gallery, for no particular reason' (P:200; C:193). Aimless again. After wandering around vaguely he remembers there are Buddha statues in another room:

> I sought them out, and suddenly I knew that this was why I had come. This was the no-reason that had brought me here.
>
> The Buddha sat facing me, carved in smooth white stone. Poised and perfect he sat, all grace and ease of bearing, the source and sustainer of the universe. His smile seemed ancient, like something I had known forever, but long long forgotten.

Existence is suffering. Its cause is desire.

[...] And here [the Buddha] was in Glasgow [...] Behind
the Buddha's head, out through the window, were trees and
a lamp-post, a glimpse of buildings against a grey Glasgow
sky. Here.

[...] I bowed to the Buddha and made my way out, through
the revolving doors, out again into the street ... (P:200–1;
C:193–4)

The bow is a bow of acceptance, of recognition of the truth
of the Buddha's unspoken 'message' that there is a way
to deal with the fact that life is full of suffering and pain.
He already knew the third and fourth Noble Truths intel-
lectually, but something in the poise of the Buddha statue
affects him on a much deeper level. Again, it speaks to his
condition. Someone else standing beside him might not
have felt the same, might not have needed that message at
that time.

In 'Changes' the point of the encounter with the Buddha is
that it is a moment of awareness, of 'getting back' to something. In many Eastern philosophies 'getting back' is the
metaphor used to describe a movement towards some kind of
equilibrium or centre, a place of balance from which one can
move easily and effectively because one's mind is untroubled
by doubt or by intellectual anxiety. It is this poise that is revealed by the Buddha's open, relaxed posture.

The story finishes with another example of openness when
the narrator goes to talk to the writer friend (probably based
on the writer Tom McGrath) who 'had taught me mantras,
loaned me books on meditation'. In other words, someone on
the same wavelength. Unfortunately Tommy is out but his
young daughter is there and in her innocence the narrator
finds another simple example of the openness of spirit that
he has been lacking. Instead of being frustrated at missing
Tommy he spends some time talking to the girl and in doing
so and unselfconsciously paying attention to her he moves
beyond the anxieties that had been troubling him. This simple interaction between human beings is something that is
sorely lacking in our selfish ego-obsessed world.

Paying attention, being mindful of others is a Buddhist attitude so it appears that the encounter with the image of the
Buddha has effected a change for the better in the narrator's
sense of his own life. This does not mean that he is 'enlightened' or has grown wise: it simply means he is on the right
path which I think is why the story ends with the simple
interaction with the child. Such moments of awareness come
and go and we should accept them and let them inform our
actions and behaviour but we should not hang on to them.

The literature of the Eastern 'ways of liberation', particularly Buddhism, is full of enlightenment stories. The starting
point of Buddhism, of course, is the Buddha's own enlightenment and Zen Buddhism with its focus on moments of *kensho*
or *satori* is especially rich in stories centred on such moments of insight. They are often intensely dramatic as if to
emphasise the suddenness of it all, but they can be puzzling
and confusing because there often seems very little connection between the events described and the sudden access of
vision.

Spence's own examples often appear to be quieter, less
dramatic, than many of the classic examples. Often they reflect a quieter, sadder awareness of the fragility of life and
so seem more emotional. Some classic enlightenment stories,
however, are described in language that suggests the intense
emotional upheaval involved even though the outward circumstances are in no way exceptional.

'Blue'

The story 'Blue' is also about a moment of vision. It is a story
based around the death of Spence's mother, one of the forma-
tive experiences of his life. The narrator goes back in time to
'when he was eleven' and tells us of that devastating event.
Like 'Tinsel' at the beginning of the book it uses the simple
words and rhythms of a child's speech, and shows the same
intense focus on apparently trivial things, such as the photographs of the Rangers football team he pastes into his scrap-
book, or the memory of 'singin the blues' with his friend Jim
at the Life Boys concert. The words of the song are sad, but
somehow 'it didn't feel sad to sing it'. (P:228; C:219)

The events of the story, however, are momentous as the boy describes the night his mother died. If the narrator is the same boy as the boy in 'Tinsel' we already know how close he is to his mother, how close he is to both parents in fact, so the pain of the loss is felt sharply. He tells of seeing his mother being carried down the tenement stairs on a stretcher and states bleakly, 'That was the last time I ever saw her'. (P:228; C:219)

When his father comes back later and tells him his mother is dead he experiences a confusing mixture of emotions:

> It was as if part of me already knew and accepted, but part of me cried out and denied it. I cried into my pillow and a numbness came on me, shielding me from the real pain. I was lying there, sobbing, but the other part of me, the part that accepted, simply looked on. I was watching myself crying, watching my puny grief from somewhere above it all. I was me and I was not-me. (P:229; C:219)

The strange unreality of it continues as he is sharply aware of life going on all around him while his mother is no longer there. Like everyone he is struck by the mystery of this and it opens him up to another insight. Looking out on the dreary world of the back courts he is depressed by it all until he becomes aware of the breeze that is blowing around him:

> It touched my cheek [...] In its warmth there was something gentle and soft, something infinitely tender. It touched all things and they moved to the one rhythm. It was almost sad, but behind the sadness was the faintest of smiles. I trembled on the edge of something eternal. The one flow. The warm breeze. My mother. All of it. (P:229–30; C:220)

The insight is comforting for the boy as the softness and tenderness of the wind as it touches him suggests that in some way his mother is still there but has become part of something bigger. The moment also highlights areas of tension and confusion in his life. The idea of his parents as individual beings separate from himself has been difficult for him to accept, especially the fact of their having a sex life. We have to remember that children in the 1950s would not have had any formal sex education in school, and that sexuality was not the common currency of the popular media that it is now. Knowledge of sexual matters was often picked up casually and confusingly from slightly older school friends. Confusion about, and fear of, sexuality, however, is something that is probably common to all young people at the time of puberty. The narrator now seems to have come to terms with his new awareness, and it can be seen as part of a normal growing-up process but it had not been easy:

> For a while after that I had been doubtful of my parents. There was this feeling that somehow they had betrayed me. But that had passed. (P:229; C:220)

It has passed because the gaining of this knowledge was a rite of passage. Like all of us he learns to assimilate it, and realises that he too is a separate individual.

The confusion though is real, and links to other areas of confusion. We have already seen him perplexed by realising that you can sing the blues and be happy at the same time. He is confused too by the fact that in a city divided by religion and football his team's colour, blue, is the colour Catholic friends tell him is the special colour associated with Mary, the Mother of God. Confusion reigns also on the emotionally-charged day of the funeral when during a moment of utterly overwhelming sadness connected with the memory of his mother he finds himself laughing almost uncontrollably at his father stepping into the bucket of water he had been using to wash the windows in preparation for funeral visitors. A Laurel and Hardy moment. The conflicting emotions are almost too strong for him to comprehend.

In the bleak time after the funeral itself he finds himself outside on his own staring at the sky:

I don't know what I had expected. A sign. Jesus to come
walking out of the close and tell me everything was all
right. A window in the sky to open and God to lean out and
say that my mother had arrived safe.

I looked up at the sky, trying to lose myself in the shift-
ing of the clouds. I focused on the shapes, willing them to
change into something I could grasp. I half-closed my eyes.
I could almost see a cross.

A dog barked and I looked around me. Everyone was
crossing the road, going into our close. I looked back to the
sky. The clouds had moved on and changed again. Through
them I could see, for a moment, a patch of clear blue. (P:231;
C:222)

Later he tells his cousin that he had 'seen her, dressed all
in blue, Our Lady, the Mother of God, in the sky above our
house'. (P:231; C:222)

The vision is comforting to the boy in the story but as
Spence has written it here it seems to involve a great deal of
wishful thinking on the boy's part – so much so that we feel
sorry for him having to deal with his devastating grief by
making up comforting stories based on an illusion. The boy
himself seems to realise that he is possibly deluding himself
and even ridicules his childish wishes himself.

In an interview with Catherine Deveney for *Scotland on
Sunday* (8th September, 2002) Spence indicates that the
reality of the moment was much simpler and much more life-
changing. In the literary form of the story he exploits the
boy's willingness to create for himself the illusion of spiritual
comfort in such a way that the reader is made to question
its value. Looking back on the actual moment in his own life
when he saw that patch of blue he says:

It was a spiritual awakening, a knowledge that there's more
than this physical body. A sense of something vast. A sense
that there is something in all of us that really doesn't die,
that really is immortal.

There is no willed belief here, nor any attempt to convince or convert anyone else: it is the simple fact of what he experienced on the day of his mother's funeral. It was obviously a pivotal moment in his life and, as Deveney goes on to suggest, the openness it engendered lies behind all of his writing.

Notes

1 *Scottish Writers Talking 2*. Murray, Isobel (ed.), East Linton: Tuckwell Press, 2002, p185

2 *Writers in Scotland*. Norris, Fiona (ed.), London: Hodder and Stoughton, 1994, p1

3 Ibid., p8

4 Ibid., p8

3. WAY TO GO

Introduction

After *Its Colours They Are Fine*, Spence published his first novel *The Magic Flute* in 1990, and another collection of stories, *Stone Garden* in 1995. *The Magic Flute* follows the lives of four boys from Glasgow whose lives all take very different paths. *Stone Garden* alternates new and previously uncollected stories, but like *The Magic Flute* it too shows an interest in different and, for Spence, more exotic settings. It includes stories set in the Caribbean, in Italy and in Japan. Both books retain a strong Glasgow flavour but by putting his characters in new and more colourful settings Spence can be seen to be deliberately extending his scope as a writer of prose fiction.

Way to Go (1998) is his second novel. It is less dense than *The Magic Flute* and has a much quicker pace than the earlier novel, perhaps indicating that Spence had learned a lot from the very act of writing his first novel where the demands of the four linked narratives were much greater than the shorter single narrative lines of his short stories. The quest theme runs right through Spence's writing and is used to good effect in *Way to Go* where the first-person narrator, Neil McGraw, attempts to find an answer to the biggest question in our lives: 'What happens when we die?' The chapters are separated by brief versions of answers to this question; quotations from the literature of East and West, Zen death verses, famous last words. Interesting in themselves, these quotations also comment on the 'meaning' of the book. So, despite beginning in the naturalistic style of *Its Colours They Are Fine*, the centrality of this question, this quest, pushes the novel very quickly into the realm of myth or fable. This is seen most obviously in Chapter One where the narrator goes from person to person asking his question. (See especially pp.13–17). A possible model for this might be Robert Louis Stevenson's *Fables*[1] which Spence discovered through reading R.H. Blyth's *Zen in English Literature and Oriental Classics*. Stevenson was one of the writers Spence included in his series of lectures on Zen in

Scottish Literature at the University of Edinburgh in 1991. With his grounding in Eastern philosophy and in the practice of meditation Spence might also describe the book as a 'teaching story' like those of the great Sufi tradition, those Zen stories where disciples ask the master how to find enlightenment, or closer to home, the parables of Jesus. The idea also reverberates through the novel in Neil's father's droll, Scottish, 'You have to learn'.

INTERPRETATIVE SUMMARY

Chapter One

This chapter introduces us to the narrator and his circumstances. He is the teenage son of respected local undertaker, Alexander (Sandy) McGraw. His mother had died in giving birth to him so he has always felt blighted, a feeling not helped by his father balefully referring to him as 'the child in question' when telling him about his mother's death. Instead of supporting his son, Sandy McGraw seems incapable of demonstrating affection or love for him. Because of this their relationship is very rocky, and clearly echoes other difficult father/son relationships in Scottish novels such as those in Stevenson's *Weir of Hermiston*, John McDougall Hay's *Gillespie* and Neil Gunn's *The Serpent*. Neil is picked on at school for being 'different', no doubt appearing to others to be a bit 'creepy' because of his background, and many references are made to his house being like something out of the cult television show *The Addams Family*. The book opens with Neil having been locked in the basement with the coffins because he had lost his school cap. This was regarded by his father as a suitable punishment.

Neil is also socially inept and a bit of a loner, perhaps due to growing up without a female presence in the house. The thing that sets him apart most, however, is probably his fascination with what happens after we die. If he mentioned this to others, it would appear morbid and completely at odds with the interests of most teenagers of the time. Even if he did not mention it, his obvious preoccupation with it would make him seem distant and 'strange'.

Regarded as weird at school he becomes friends with another outsider, the Indian girl Padma who is an outsider
because of her colour and her culture. Padma introduces him
to Indian food, vegetarianism, and to the concept of *karma*,
the Hindu/Buddhist idea that what happens to you in the
future depends on what you do now. As Padma says:

> 'It's a kind of law. Means everybody gets what's coming to
> them, one way or another.' (p.24)

Padma, whose name means Lotus, acts with grace and
gentleness in the face of much provocation, an attitude which
makes a huge impression on Neil although he finds it hard to
behave that way himself. She gives him a first glimpse of a
way of thinking which will be important to him later. In the
end, however, she too is constrained by the circumstances of
her own background and upbringing, although she describes
this as her *karma*. She moves away to Bradford to an ar-
ranged marriage, leaving Neil isolated and alone except for
his father.

Once again his life seems empty and pointless. This is
emphasised in a short section on pp.28–29 where his father
comes home from the pub, not drunk but in a strange mood.
Each of his father's short statements seems to give a bleaker
and bleaker vision of life as a meaningless journey towards
the final mystery of death:

> 'Whatever way you look at it, it's a long walk off a short
> plank. And the long and the short of it is, we die. End of
> story. Bottom Line. We die.' (p.29)

He reduces the rough poetry of this by finishing with the
simple Scottish expression of frustration and hopelessness,
'Ach'. For Sandy McGraw that is all there is to say. Life has
defeated him and all he can do is shake his head and mutter.
It is an all-too-common gesture.

Throughout this early part of the book Neil's father is por-
trayed as dour, harsh and miserable. He is a drinker who
turns maudlin or vicious by turns when he has been drink-

ing. Locking Neil in the cellar store-room with the coffins is part of this and cannot but remind us of the orphaned Oliver Twist sleeping among the coffins in the undertaker Sowerberry's workshop in Dickens' novel. Yet Neil is not an orphan, and after his father's death comes to realise that his ill-treatment of his son stemmed largely from human weakness and frailty, his inability to cope with life after the death of his wife. Gradually we learn to see his father not just as a domestic tyrant but as a man struggling to understand his life and to find a way through it. Shakespeare's King Lear spoke of 'poor suffering humanity' and, as Neil quickly learns from his study of Hindu and Buddhist thought, the first part of the Buddha's Four Noble Truths is that 'all life is suffering'. The second part of the Buddha's message, however, is that the way to deal with this situation is to extend compassion to all sentient beings because everyone is suffering and everyone needs help and support and kindness to live well.

The chapter ends where it began with Neil in a coffin in the cellar, but this time he has chosen to be there because he 'wanted to imagine it, the real thing'. (p.29) If it is real then how can it be imagined? Spence the novelist is perhaps suggesting that life only becomes real when we engage with it imaginatively. Neil seems to have reached a point where he stops asking others for the answer to his question, and tries to find out for himself. This is what he does when he kicks off his sandshoes, climbs in and lies down still and quiet.

> Close my eyes. Feel the breathing, the heartbeat. They would stop, like that. I'd be stiff and cold. I shivered. Only I wouldn't feel it, wouldn't know. Hard to imagine nothing. [...]
>
> I'd see nothing, not even this red behind my eyelids. I'd be deaf and dumb, taste and smell nothing. Feel nothing. Not be this body. Then I'd think nothing, know nothing. No mind. I would *be* nothing.
>
> It only seemed a moment, but it happened. Not a dream, it was real. I was suddenly floating above myself, disembodied, looking down. Saw the wee figure [...] stretched out, the jeans and t-shirt, the bare feet. That was me. But so was this up here flying free. [...] I looked down again at

myself still lying there, saw my sandshoes and socks where
I'd dropped them [...] and it all seemed wonderfully funny,
a joke. And just as quick I was back down inside the wee
body, back in this me.

I sat up laughing, astonished. Looked at my hands, wig-
gled my toes. *Ha!* Something in me was not this, was more.
(pp.29–30)

His response to this realisation, then, is profoundly different
from his father's exhausted and despairing 'Ach'.

The 'vision' takes the form of what has become known as a
near-death experience where people who have been involved
in an accident or who have had a serious operation in hospital describe floating above their own body and looking down
on the scene from above. Sometimes their attention is drawn
to a tunnel with bright lights that seem to beckon them to
enter the tunnel. People who describe this experience turn
back before reaching the lights and the experience itself is
unverifiable by others. For most people who have this experience it seems not to be frightening at all.

For Neil McGraw too the experience holds no fear, and we
should remember that as a narrator he has revealed a great
deal of his own doubt and fear, his sense of being somehow
inadequate, so he is not hiding his fear from the reader. The
result of his meditation, for in essence that is what it is, is
to realise that he is much more than his physical body, an
insight that brings him joy and delight.

I sat up laughing, astonished. Looked at my hands, wig-
gled my toes. *Ha!* Something in me was not this, was more.
(p.30)

In a sense this is the answer to his question, 'What happens when we die?' You merge with something much greater
than your own sense of self, go back to 'from where you came'.
This answer chimes with the Hindu and Buddhist ideas that
Padma had told Neil about, and they also chime with the
teachings of Sri Chinmoy. Yet Spence shows this insight
coming to a teenage boy in Glasgow. It is available to every-

body if they could only see it, could only learn to look in the right way, so that they recognise the answer when it is given. He is also clear that such glimpses of understanding are not once-and-for-all events. The rest of the book shows this basic insight being doubted, forgotten and tested over and over again, with Neil's understanding of it gradually deepening as he gets older and becomes more fully engaged with the life of his community, rather than being so self-absorbed.

Chapter Two
Chapter Two shows Neil growing into adolescence and becoming rebellious. His own lack of sympathy and tolerance helps to make his home life with his father even more difficult, while school 'was a zone of hell' (p.35) as his oddness and the other students' knowledge of his background made his life almost unbearable. He does not 'fit', and his preoccupation with death and what happens after you die makes it even harder for him to fit into a world where people try to ignore the existence of suffering and death. There are many good and natural reasons for this but Neil is unable to share them. He is driven to wrestle with this question. Perhaps it is his *karma*. Perhaps at some deep level the implication that he is responsible for his mother's death lies behind this, especially as his father did nothing to assuage his feelings of guilt and anxiety:

> I remembered asking my father when I was wee. What happened to her? And he'd struggled with how to answer, what to say, had finally come out with it.
> 'She died in childbirth. The child in question being you.'
> (p.13)

Chapter Two also sees Neil becoming more involved in the family business as he is asked by his father to help at the funeral of Rab Deans' father. This is awkward for him as Deans had picked on him when he was still at school. He is also included by his father in a demonstration of the art of embalming which is the latest thing in the undertaking world, something his father sees as an opportunity to devel-

op his business and improve on the service he provides. The
embalming process is demonstrated by a man from Kirkcaldy whom Neil immediately nicknames the Wraith Rover
in recognition of his imagined connection with Kirkcaldy's
football team Raith Rovers. 'Wraith' means 'ghost', so the
pun again draws attention to Neil's rather facetious attitude
to his father's business, the very serious business of death
and dying. He hates the embalming process because the end
result is a gruesome parody of rude good health as the face is
plumped up and given a rosy pink glow through the injection
of a dye under the skin. He finds this deeply troubling and is
unable to accept his father's view that it makes things more
bearable for distressed loved ones. Once again he retreats
into a kind of childish humour which is a genuine defence
mechanism, but one which blocks any deepening of insight
into the reality of death and what it means to himself and
to others.

One result of Spence's use of first-person narration is to
highlight Neil McGraw's selfishness and self-obsession –
qualities that prevent him from feeling any sympathy for his
father. Sandy McGraw is obviously not an ideal parent and
treats his son with little respect or understanding, but Neil's
response to this is to be just as dour and thrawn as his father
himself in his interactions with him.

If Neil's life-quest is to find out what happens when we
die, as the son of an undertaker, being trained to help in
and then (presumably) take over the business, he seems to
be ideally placed to find an answer to his question. Yet he
is determined not to have anything to do with his father or
his work. It is a common feeling among teenagers. Andy, his
father's driver, points this out:

> 'It's natural,' he said. 'My two are the same wi me. I canny
> talk to them. They just don't want to know. So don't be too
> hard on your da. He's toiling as well.' (p.54)

In the same conversation Andy gives Neil (and the reader) a
different perspective on his father:

'He was always a bit dour. But there wasn't so much darkness about him when your mother was alive. He took that
hard, her going so young [...] He had to get somebody else
in to handle the arrangements. Couldn't face it. Might have
been better if he had.' (pp.54–55)

Andy is here speaking plainly in the language of an ordinary working man, but his words are full of an understanding and compassion that is completely lacking in Neil at this
point. As one of those of whom Neil asks his question Andy
is an important character in the book. Neil himself says he is
uncomfortable listening to Andy's explanation and does not
really take it in. He feels 'out of [his] depth'. (p.55)

Auld Jack the joiner also gives Neil a different perspective
on his father, beginning by describing Sandy McGraw's trou-
bled relationship with his own father, Neil's grandfather:
'Your da's all sweetness and light compared to his da'. (p.55)
He also explains that the undertaking job was not for him
although he had helped out from time to time. For Jack the
hard part of the job was 'all the business of consoling people.
Keeping up that front all the time'. (p.56) The implication
is that Neil's father is good at this. It is a skill that requires
sensitivity and thoughtfulness, qualities that seem in short
supply in his relationship with his son.

In a conversation with his father Neil seems to see this as
somehow false, or hypocritical, a put-on kindness, 'just part
of the job'. (p.43) His father explains that when he had asked
Neil to help at the funeral of Rab Deans' father he did this so
that Rab would have someone of his own age to talk to at the
funeral, to help put him at ease during a difficult time. Neil
is aggressively dismissive that undertakers could 'Switch it
on and off just like that'. (p.43) His father's reply silences
him:

'Listen, son.' The patient voice, infuriating. 'In this game
you've got to learn a kind of professional detachment. Like
being a doctor. If you let yourself get too involved with people's suffering, it'll drive you right up the wall.'

> I was about to bat back some smart reply, but the look in
> his eyes stopped me. He'd been through it, been drawn into
> that unremitting grief, again and again, had learned to deal
> with it [...] His eyes glazed over again. The look had passed,
> a glimpse in. It made me feel tense in my stomach. (p.43)

Again we see a turning away, an inability to accept the difficult insight. Ironically it is Neil's father who understands
the difficulty of understanding the mystery of death and the
way we must put it to the back of our minds if we are to
live 'normally'. When Neil comments on how Deans has been
changed by his encounter with death, his father says quite
simply but eloquently, 'Bereavement can do that [...] Open
folks' eyes. For a while.' (p.44) Caught up in his own ego, his
own 'issues', Neil had been unable to see this.

After this brief moment when he and his father almost
understand each other, a moment that could have led to a
degree of reconciliation, Neil's thoughtless behaviour causes
a permanent rift between them. In an episode that melo-
dramatically links love and death with a rather edgy black
humour, Neil's father comes back early from the pub to find
Neil and a girl he has met at a party making love in a coffin
in the cellar. This is the final straw for his father and their
relationship deteriorates into icy silence and a barely con-
cealed contempt for one another until the night when Neil
locks his drunken father in the cellar in a coffin, neatly reminding us of the opening sentence of the novel ('I sat up in
the coffin reading a comic and eating a sherbet fountain').
This shows that it is now Neil who is the dominant figure in
their relationship. He has grown up, is his own person, is no
longer there to be controlled by his father. But, as the rest of
the novel attests, there is still a lot of growing up to do.

Chapter Three
The quest theme becomes more prominent again as Neil
moves away from home as soon as he can and follows the
traditional path to London where the streets are paved with
possibilities, if not with gold. It is a London that Spence also
describes in stories like 'Bland Umbrellas' in *Stone Garden*,

a London of hippy squats, wholefood restaurants, and end-
less vague discussions of Zen Buddhism and Eastern religion
and philosophy. It is the time of *The Whole Earth Catalog*, a
time of great optimism for the young who felt that the rigid-
ity of a corrupt and immoral Establishment could be pulled
down and replaced with alternative lifestyles. For a young
boy from Glasgow it is an intoxicating new way of life now
that he has broken free of the constraints of his miserable
life with his father. Neil enters into the life of this brave new
world with naïve optimism but learns a great deal from the
experience.

Having no communication with his father or with anyone
else from his old life he is free to explore the world anew.
His first response to finding himself accepted is typically im-
mature: 'This was the hippy trip I'd read about. Crash pads
and communes. Mindblowing peace and love. Cool.' (p.78).
It doesn't seem quite so cool when he realises that his new
friend Abe Morris who tells him all about the Sufi concept
of *karass,* the idea that everyone we meet is somehow connected to us and that we have something to learn from them,
has picked him up for sex. It is to Neil's credit that he is able
to deal with this situation maturely. He declines the offer but
remains friendly with Abe who, for all his charlatanism and
blarney, does become an important figure in Neil's life: part
of his *karass,* with much to teach him.

Like *The Magic Flute,* Chapter Three is full of references
and allusions to the music and the attitudes of the time. It
is 1969 and Neil attends the famous concert in Hyde Park
where The Rolling Stones mourned the recent death of their
guitarist, Brian Jones. Film footage of the event shows Mick
Jagger reading part of a poem by the English Romantic poet
Shelley before a cloud of butterflies is released over the heads
of the crowd to symbolise the freeing of the human soul from
its earthly bondage. The gesture is brief and fleeting as the
band then move into an earthy performance of many of their
greatest hits.

His time in London culminates in two important events,
a bad drug trip, and the untimely death of Abe who has
taken on the role of mentor to the young Scotsman. Both

events are disturbing and shock Neil further out of his thoughtlessness.

Under the influence of a psychedelic drug Neil seems to go beyond the surface reality of where he is 'to a different realm.' (p.96) He finds himself wandering in a strange landscape haunted by a dark figure who keeps moving just out of sight when he tries to focus on it.

> Then I found myself in front of a wooden structure, a boat that had been washed up on the shore, half buried in the sand, its ribs and spars sticking up. I crawled inside it, lay down on my back, was aware of my own ribs, my skeleton, cage of bone containing me. Felt myself abandoned there, washed up, bones picked clean, the wind blowing through. What happens when you die. Skull filled with sand.
>
> I sat up, was myself again, not dead. I pressed my head with my hands, felt the skull beneath the skin. I was laughing/crying. This wee body. Me. I lay down again, curled up. Felt the thud of my heart, pulse beating through me, lifeblood. I wanted to drift again, float, but I was closed in, constricted, pressure crushing me. My head and my body were gripped, stuck. A long time trapped. No way out. I had to get out, I couldn't move. I had to get out, push through. I remembered this. Darkness and pain. A taste like metal, like blood. (p.96)

This passage is full of literary allusions (to T.S. Eliot, to John Webster, to the Border Ballads, to Samuel Beckett) but its sheer physical sense of entrapment comes through powerfully. A few pages later it becomes clearer that what Neil has experienced is a kind of flashback to his difficult birth. He seems to remember being stuck in the birth canal, and goes on to say:

> I was the child in question. The foetus curled in the skeleton's womb. That taste like metal like blood. Astride of the grave and a difficult birth. I had killed my mother. (p.101)

The disturbing nature of this experience seems to give him more understanding of his father who must also have felt guilty about the manner of his wife's death. The experience also seems to steady him a bit in his drifting, rootless London life and he takes on regular work and begins to learn how to be a cook. This is a job that will allow him to travel but also makes him a useful member of society, someone who has something to give.

The death of Abe in a senseless accident makes Neil realise how fragile life is and how suddenly death can strike. It is another important lesson for him. It teaches him sharply about transience and mortality. Abe's unconventional funeral also foreshadows Neil's later work as a funeral director with a difference.

Chapter Four
Chapter Four comes right at the heart of the novel and marks a great turning point in Neil's life. His quest continues after Abe's death when he sets off on fifteen years of travel. It is a time of learning, and a brief comment at the beginning of the chapter calls into question a great deal of what passes for learning in the modern western world:

> I kept travelling for fifteen weird years. Passed myself off as a cook and learned as I went. Picked up enough to survive and move on. Kept asking the unanswerable, repeating it. My mantra, or koan more like. What happens when you die? (p.121)

Learning here is not a matter of learning enough information to pass exams and gaining a certificate for regurgitating that information: it is about learning practical skills and developing mastery of those skills. Behind it all lies the big question which Neil asks as 'What happens when you die?' but which could just as easily be framed as 'What does it mean to be alive?' because to understand the meaning of death is to learn to appreciate life much more fully before you die, to appreciate those around you fully before they die. Much traditional western education does not attempt to deal with these questions, which are surely the most fundamental questions we can ask. Our whole modern way of life

wants to avoid thinking about them. Yet the question lies at
the heart of much modern literature. Samuel Beckett's play
Waiting for Godot, for instance, is on one level an account
of how we will do anything to avoid thinking about the nature of our existence. The characters Vladimir and Estragon
in their stripped-down bare world are ideally placed to face
these questions, but spend their time instead finding ways
to 'pass the time'. It seems that nowadays we pass our time
in this world living as if we are going to live forever. In some
ways this is sensible as constantly thinking about death is
morbid and debilitating.

On the other hand, not thinking about death, not being
aware of it, is to ignore one of the most important facts of our
lives. Other times and other cultures have been more aware
of the way life and death intertwine and how they are two
sides of the same process. *Yin* and *yang*. Hamish Henderson's
poem 'The Flyting o' Life and Daith' makes the same point
from within the Scottish tradition, while the Border ballads
in general often make us aware of the insubstantiality of the
barrier between the worlds of the living and the dead. Robert
Burns, too, in the poem 'Death and Doctor Hornbook' had
his narrator sit down for a blether with a weary Death who
complains of the town's new doctor who is making things
hard for him. As a young boy growing up in Glasgow, Spence
himself may have been aware of the brooding presence of the
city's vast Victorian Necropolis, a city of the dead.

Neil's years of travelling, another part of the 'hippy trip' of
the 1960s and early 1970s, bring him into contact with many
of these different cultures. Two things are striking here. He
is still an obsessive character whose intense driven-ness to
seek answers to his question marks him out as *different*.
Like the boy of Chapters One and Two, he does not really fit
in with the normal social world around him. His life seems
lacking in balance, and he seems unfulfilled. He is uncomfortable in his own skin in a way that is unhealthy in that
it prevents him from moving on, opening out and becoming
productive.

The other important point is the way that Chapter Four
picks up and develops the fable form from Chapter One. This

time, instead of asking his questions directly of those around him, he visits different cultures and explores their burial customs and their attitudes to death in order to get closer to the answer he seeks. The chapter describes the Mexican Day of the Dead, a sectarian funeral in Ireland, a Balinese cremation, the burial ghats of the Ganges. From each of these experiences he gains valuable insights into the very different ways other cultures think about death.

He also sees an old man drop dead in front of him on a New York Street. The man approaches him to beg for money:

> Saw him out of the corner of my eye, a figure stepping towards me out of a doorway. First instinct was to step aside, speed up. Hey, this was New York. Head down keep moving don't make eye-contact. Then he made a noise, a gasped-out cry and I stopped and looked and he stared right at me, right into me. (pp.123–4)

The man collapses and dies right there in front of him and the incident is shocking. However, it is noticeable that, although Neil's selfish attitude of non-involvement with those around him is challenged and the look given by the old man seems to pierce his psychic armour for a brief moment, his lack of emotional involvement in the death of this human being is striking. The man's death quickly becomes just another piece of information to file away with the other 'answers' to his question.

Later, on a visit back to London, Des, a friend from his squatting days, sums it up:

> 'Is it just me?' I asked Des [...] 'I mean, is it selective perception sort of thing? Do I run into all this stuff about death and funerals because I'm looking for it?'
>
> [...] 'Of course it's you,' he said. 'You're a morbid bastard, a fucking ghoul. Spectre at the fucking feast.'
>
> Cheers. (p.130)

Having to ask the question shows a lack of self-knowledge despite the fact that he has learned so much from being on his quest. It seems, though, that this knowledge is useless and pointless because it has not yet been internalised, has not yet become part of who Neil is and how he lives. It is still somehow external to him.

Things begin to change during the time he spends at Varanasi on the banks of the Ganges, the sacred river of India. The scene is one that takes place among some of the more gruesome (to Western eyes) burial customs, as the bodies of the dead are cremated beside the river and their ashes cast upon the water of the holy river so that they can become free from the eternal round of life and death, as this is a society for whom reincarnation is a reality, not a possibility. Some bodies, for instance those of children and holy men, are not cremated but simply placed in the water.

> Funeral pyres blazing at dusk on the burning-ghats of the Ganges, the holy city of Varanasi, once Benares. A woman wailing, screaming, being led away by friends. Packs of jackals snuffling around, vultures circling, lazy. A solitary figure crosslegged in meditation, among the ashes, the powdered bone and charred wood. He was naked except for a loincloth, hair long and matted, body smeared with ash. Sat unmoving, unmoved. (p.133)

The Christian burial service as it appears in *The Book Of Common Prayer* contains the lines, 'ashes to ashes, dust to dust' but the very beauty of that carefully cadenced phrasing which soothes the bereaved by its consoling rhythms and the sense of the body's decay taking place over a long stretch of time so that it is part of a natural process, diverts our awareness from the visceral reality of death and decay. What Neil faces at Varanasi is just that physical reality: the burning meat smell, the *sadhus* or holy men sitting among the ashes of the dead grinding their bones into dust. It is very different from anything he had seen when helping his father, but it is important to remember that the one person who gave him a straight answer to his question 'What happens when you die?' was his father who focused very deliberately on the physical nature of the body's decomposition. His account is so direct that Neil throws up, can't deal with it. His father's final comment is a very dry, Scottish 'You did ask.' (pp. 16–17)

For the *sadhus* of Varanasi, meditation in the place of death, with the bodies of the dead all around them, is a way to discover what it means to die and so what it means to live. In Varanasi it seems that Neil is now able to deal with the physical reality of death. After all his evasions, it is as if he has finally found a place where he fits in, a 'howling no-place of jackals and hungry ghosts [a Buddhist term denoting those still tortured by their desires] [...] this place of skulls, bones picked clean, reduced to dust, dispersed.' (p.135) The *sadhu* tells him that if he sits in meditation in this place he will find his own answer to his question, and that no-one else can answer it for him. The *sadhu* himself has had glimpses and glimmers of an answer from Yamaraj, the Lord of Death, and the goddess Kali, who has shown him compassion. Neil's answer comes in an unexpected way, as it should because, if we can dictate what is acceptable to us as an answer, then we are still operating out of a selfish egocentric vision of the world.

He tries to sit in meditation with the *sadhu*, trying to focus at last on his quest, on his *koan*, and is almost defeated by the experience which is profoundly disturbing:

> Had to stay awake for fear I'd be engulfed [...] never wake up again, be nothing. Be one more corpse in this place of skulls [...]
>
> I kept drifting, jerking awake, lost all sense of myself. Shadows, forms, coalesced, took shape, came at me out the dark. Monkey-demons, birds, wraiths [...] One slouched figure I knew brushed past and stood behind me, chilled and numbed me, froze me right through. The Reaper [...]
>
> Grey halflight and the sadhu still sitting. I huddled arms round my knees, couldn't sit upright. Everything hurt. I curled up among the ashes on the hard ground. A momentary acid flashback, foetus in a cage of bone. Then nothing.
>
> Nothing. (p.135)

The reference to 'this place of skulls' is quite literal, but to a Christian reader also has echoes of Golgotha, the hill where Jesus was crucified. His meditation takes him to a place where nothing makes sense any more, where he can barely think, where everything he believed in before or thought he understood before has dissolved. It reminds us too of the Buddha's enlightenment under the Bo tree. Like the Buddha, Neil has arrived at a state of abject despair. Because of this the wheel begins to turn and his life starts to change.

A woman in a sari approaches him, at first appearing like another vision or hallucination, 'some trick of the light', but gradually he realises she is a real woman. He feels he has known her before. She brings him water and that simple act of kindness seems to bring him back to life. Then, guided by the woman, the first thing he does is to pass on the kindness by sharing the water with the *sadhu*. Two small things echo each other here. When the woman asks Neil if he is English he immediately makes it clear that he is Scottish, then laughs at the fact that even in this ultimate place he is still making distinctions, still thinking dualistically, a way of thinking that he should now realise is limiting and reductive. He also shows that he has not really moved beyond this way of thinking when he notes the incongruity of pouring the water from a modern plastic bottle into the begging bowl the *sadhu* had had made out of the skull of a friend. The *sadhu,* on the other hand, simply accepts the water and bows in recognition of the kindness. Kindness is a key concept for Spence. It is the antidote to much of the violence and thoughtlessness that he documents in modern life. The painter Carlo puts it best in the story 'Milan Cathedral At The Bottom Of The Sea' in Spence's collection *Stone Garden* when he talks about the struggle of living an ordinary, decent life against a background of strikes and social unrest: 'This is the struggle. To make something. To be a little kind ...' (p.86)

The woman's name is Lila, which means something like 'the divine dance of the cosmos'. In other words she appears in the novel as a real person who brings love and a female presence into the life of the social misfit Neil McGraw, but at the same time she also functions as an image of non-dual thinking for she is also a manifestation of Kali, the goddess of compassion. The *sadhu*, too, had known her before. For Hindus life is often imaged as a divine dance, or the continual play of opposites. Most Westerners are aware of this concept through the Chinese Taoist *yin-yang* symbol which also images the way opposites continually merge and morph and change into and out of one another. The non-dual way of thinking acknowledges the opposition but does not attempt to say that one thing is better than the other. Rather it suggests that we will only retain sanity and achieve wisdom if we use our awareness to understand the change and interaction between them. To this way of thinking death is not the negation of life but another aspect of a dynamic process.

The real woman, Lila, is sensual and attractive and a genuine relationship develops between them. In her quiet gracefulness she calls to mind Padma, the Indian girl who had befriended Neil at school in Chapter One, and told him about *karma*. She has a profound effect on Neil and after a time follows him to London where they marry. This is a huge change for Neil. He seems here to become softer and more human simply by being involved in a loving relationship which takes him out of his selfishness and self-obsession. It also leads to renewed contact with his father when he telephones to tell him about the wedding. It is a tense telephone call full of uneasy silences with Neil as taciturn as his father – although he is the one who had made the call. For all Neil's new-found humanity their conversation is bleak and depressing. Despite their long separation there seems little hope of reconciliation.

Soon after this he receives a call from Glasgow to tell him that his father has died. Neil's response is flat and unemotional, as if he does not know how to respond. What his father's death does do, however, is bring him back to Glasgow to deal with the funeral arrangements.

Chapter Five
The return is a shock to his system. In contrast to his own years of travelling and seeking and changing, his father's life had been one of living in one place and growing old and tired

in it. The very sameness and ordinariness of the house is
shocking. The contrast between the colour and excitement of
his travelling and the tawdry reality of the old house is very
strong:

> Everything was so much smaller than I remembered.
> Shrunk. [...] I turned the key and pushed open the front
> door, dragged the scatter of junkmail on the mat. And the
> smells hit me, stopped me right there and churned my guts,
> a fusty mix of dust and rot and chemicals, old waxy polish
> and stale air freshener, sick-sweet. (p.151)

A house which has grown tired by its effort to cover-up or
hide its reality, a house of the dead. It brings him face-to-
face again with that difference that set him apart as a child
and as a teenager. It also brings him face-to-face with the
reality of his father's life, and to some extent with his own
selfishness.

Moving through the house we are reminded of his response to that other house in Chapter One when he had
gone to help his father remove a body, 'the sense of that old
man's life, in the sad room, the few pathetic possessions'
(p.12). Looking at the unwashed dishes and frying pan he is
struck by the thought that his father had 'walked out that
day not knowing' (p.153). The thought disturbs him because
it is not an abstract thought, not about death as an idea but
at last for him about death as a reality that affects him directly. While Lila opens windows and curtains to let in light
and air, Neil feels claustrophobic, almost overwhelmed by
the experience so he has to get out, has to find some fresh
air. (p.153) At this crucial moment his instinct is once again
to run away.

Because of previous experiences and insights, however, he
is unable to turn away completely and, partly through the
encouragement of Lila and Andy, his father's driver, he begins to face up to the reality of where he is now, the reality
of what is actually happening here and now. He prepares
his father's body for cremation. Andy's simple words are true
and help Neil to understand what he is doing:

> 'It's good that you're doing this [...] It can't be easy when
> it's your own [...] I know you and him never saw eye to eye.
> But he wasn't a bad bloke. No better or worse than the rest
> of us.' (p.155)

Neil is beginning to understand that simple, sometimes
clichéd, words can help people to cope with the pain, the dis-
orientation of grief.

When Andy goes, Neil is left with 'what had been [his]
father' and in a description that is reminiscent of an Old
Master painting in its unflinchingly accurate detail he describes his father's body:

> The wee pale body, exposed and cold and vulnerable [...]
> Flesh slack on the skinny frame, the ribs showing through.
> The mouth slightly open, no teeth, the cheeks clapped in.
> The way he looked sometimes when he fell asleep drunk,
> paralytic. (p.156)

The vulnerability of the old man's body is striking, as is
the feeling that in seeing that vulnerability we are witness to
something intimate and private that we should not be seeing.
I think that this sense is particularly strong here because it
is his own father Neil is describing. It is the moment when he
finally sees that in some way he has taken his father's place,
the place of the man who saw Neil's own vulnerability when
he was a baby, 'the child in question'. He feels tenderly and
instinctively that despite their differences he has a duty to
care for this man who can no longer care for himself. It is the
beginning of a sense in Neil of opening up to an intensity of
emotion he has, like most of us, tried to avoid because it is so
powerful and overwhelming:

> And looking at those familiar features, I saw them much
> more like my own than I'd ever realised or admitted. One
> day this would be me. (p.156)

What he is beginning to experience is a strong sense of being connected to the rest of humanity, the realisation that

human beings do not live in isolation, but are always connected. This insight is the beginning of compassion. Spence
goes on to describe how Neil gently and tenderly cleans his
father's body 'head to toe' in such a way that the reader is
made intensely aware of the physical reality of the body. Neil
himself tries to distance himself a bit by reminding himself
that 'this was just a shell, just dead stuff [...] the old man but
not. Him but not him.' (p.157)

The attempt fails and he finds the reality of it too much for
him:

> The striplights made a faint low buzz, threw their weird
> cold light on everything, on the dead body lying there. My
> father. Dead as everybody that had ever died [...] And I
> wanted to talk to him. But how much I was saying, how
> much I just thought, God knows. (p.157)

The effect on Neil is not only psychological. When he has fin-
ished he is physically shaking.

His father's funeral is a miserable affair during which the
grim-faced minister McNaught uses the occasion to berate
him for choosing cremation instead of burial, and then em-
ploys the few words of his sermon to deliver a rant which
increases the unhappiness of the mourners. After the funeral
Andy again attempts to get Neil to see that his father, for all
their disagreements, was a decent man:

> 'Takes it out you this stuff. When the wife died, couple of
> years back, I mind when I got to this stage I just slumped.
> And I'll tell you, your old man was a great help, seeing me
> through it. Rock solid, he was. Kept me going.' (p.164)

Again Andy's apparent simplicity goes far beyond Neil's
intellectual cleverness. It makes him begin to think about
his father having to cope with the death of his young wife,
and makes him aware of a side of his parents' lives he had
never known. This is brought home to him later when he
goes through his father's things and finds an old brown envelope in which his father had kept some photographs includ-

ing his wedding photograph, 'the two of them stiff and formal
in the way of that generation, not at ease with the camera,
but smiling and so young.' (p.171) Again he notes the like-
ness between himself and his father but more importantly he
can see his father smiling and happy in a way he had never
seen before. He stares at the photographs trying to unlock
their secrets, trying to find a way to relate to the people in
them, especially his father: a picture of his father leaning on
the parapet of a bridge, another of his mother leaning in the
same way, and a third which

> [...] showed the two of them together, perhaps snapped by
> a passer-by. More relaxed than the wedding photo [...] The
> young couple, their lives ahead of them. They thought. I
> turned the picture over. On the back in fluid copperplate,
> the ink faintly brown, it read *Kelvingrove Park. June 27th
> 1950.*
>
> There were other pictures, the one I had seen as a child
> – my mother in wartime uniform, another of my parents
> dressed up at a night out, startled by the flash as they sat
> laughing, tipsy, my father with a drink in his right hand, a
> cigarette in his left.
>
> Fucksake, I heard myself say. I never knew you at all.
> (p.172)

All families until very recently had photographs like this,
even down to the faded writing on the back. The captured
fragments of a former life are very poignant and are a direct
link to the reader who not only has similar photographs of
his or her own family, but who has possibly stood on that
same bridge in Glasgow's Kelvingrove Park on a visit to the
art gallery there. Like many bereaved people Neil is becoming aware of the mystery of other people's lives.

Shortly after his father's funeral he is approached by a local
woman, Mrs Robertson, who asks him to bury her husband.
Despite his recent experience of dealing with bereavement
Neil is uncertain and is not sure whether he wants to take
on his father's business. Lila is the one who gently steers
him towards making the decision, although in a sense he

has no real choice in the matter as the community itself has decided for him by turning to him for help. Mrs Robertson approaches Neil because 'Archie always wanted your da to do it. He trusted him like. Felt safe.' (p.173) Neil himself is still rather reluctant, feels trapped by this. It is as if he is still trying to avoid being part of a community, trying to avoid being connected.

Through his involvement with Mrs Robertson, helping her with the arrangements for her husband's funeral and taking care of his body, he makes up his mind to take on the business. Involvement with Mrs Robertson also sows the seed of the idea that will come to define Neil McGraw's undertaking business and set it apart from others.

Discussing the type of coffin her husband would have wanted, they decide on a simple coffin decorated with the painted design of a ship because Archie Robertson loved boats and had worked all his days in the shipyards. This idea which will develop into a successful business venture for him is something that emerges from his involvement with others, not a clever idea thought out in isolation, although it draws on his own experiences while travelling and has echoes of the funeral of Abe in Chapter Three. In reality what he is doing is re-connecting by bringing his own experiences to his community.

The decision to follow in his father's footsteps, to take on his role and therefore something of his identity is a huge step for the rather rootless Neil McGraw. He can no longer selfishly run away from things but must now stand and face them. One of the first things he does to mark his new awareness of who he is and where he belongs is to take his father's ashes to the bridge in Kelvingrove Park he had recognised in the photograph in the old brown envelope:

> The river was slow and sluggish, yellow-brown. I tipped the urn, emptied out the ashes, watched them scatter and drift [...] to settle on the water and disappear. And I suddenly felt focused entirely on what I was doing, in the action itself. The feel of the urn. The cold of the day. Myself there in the moment. Watching the drift and flow. No thought and no feeling. Mind empty, heart still. (p.182)

For a man who has spent much of his life running away from
the awkwardness of involvement with others, except for his
relationship with Lila, this is a crucial moment:

> I suddenly felt focused entirely on what I was doing, in the
> action itself. (p.182)

In other words he is involved in his own life in a way that
he has not been before, as he has always been an observer,
an outsider, different. It is a brief moment of insight, but
Spence is keen not to make it too portentous. Some of the
ashes from the urn are blown back into Neil's face and hair
by the breeze as if to remind him that, although his father
is gone, something of him remains. The reader, of course, remembers the *sadhu* sitting at Varanasi, his body covered in
the dust and ashes of the dead.

Chapter Six
Chapter Six describes how Neil takes over and runs the family business, takes on his father's role in the community, but
offers colourful coffins based on African or Balinese ideas.
The coffins are decorated by Neil's old friend Des, who is an
artist. Neil's new publicity brochure fulfils a need in that
it provides information for the public about what happens
when someone dies but the tone of the brochure is lively and
humorous as well as being informative. It also highlights
very clearly the difference between Neil and his father and
their attitudes to death and bereavement:

> When someone close to you dies, it's a time to grieve, for
> there's nothing as deep as that pain of loss. But it's also a
> time to celebrate the person's life, give thanks for having
> known them, give them a good send-off. (p.187)

This celebratory aspect of funerals is something Neil has
witnessed on his travels and it has affected him deeply, so
that he wants to bring this attitude to Scotland where funerals have traditionally been rather grim affairs with the
emphasis on loss and grief. Neil's attitude is that we can

acknowledge the painful nature of bereavement, but that it is
crucial for those who remain to go back to their own lives feeling that they have done everything they can for the deceased
and that it is okay to carry on with their own lives. The dead
person will still be in their minds and in their hearts but they
have otherwise 'gone beyond' as the Buddhists say. Grief and
celebration are part of the same experience and so need to be
balanced. One of the most obvious models for this in Western
society can be found in the marching funerals of New Orleans
where the tradition was to accompany the body to the cem-
etery with slow, sombre music, but to play more upbeat music
on the way back from the grave. Death cannot be avoided so
what is needed is to develop a balanced attitude towards it.

The idea of creative funerals proves to be a great business
success but on a deeper level it presents the reader with an
important and awkward question: how should we treat our
dead? It is an issue we all have to deal with and Spence has
the reader nodding along quietly in agreement one minute
when a child's coffin is designed to reflect his life and his
interests in a way that seems true to how he lived. The coffin is shaped like a football boot and the boy is buried in his
football top. Fishing boats are popular and one woman wants
a coffin shaped like a subway carriage for her train driver
husband. Next minute we are shocked as someone arranges
a different kind of funeral, with a coffin shaped like a bottle for her alcoholic husband. Neil himself is shocked when
someone asks about a sky burial:

> I hoped he might mean he wanted his remains transported
> to Kyle of Lochalsh, over the sea to Skye, buried in the cem-
> etery at Portree. A Skye burial. (p.215)

The man was actually asking about the possibility of having a Tibetan sky burial, with his body being left on a plat-
form out in the open for the weather and the scavengers to
dispose of it over time. This is a step too far for Neil so that
we can see that, although he has brought ideas about death
and burial from other cultures and is challenging traditional
Western attitudes to these things, there is a sense in his own

mind about what is and is not appropriate. This is important because his new business attracts a lot of attention, one
could almost say notoriety, from the press. His sense of ap-
propriateness, however, is quite challenging for the reader
too. Some of the statements he makes to the media seem
glib or thoughtless. Despite his increasing maturity, and his
increasing sense of involvement with his community, something of his old jokey self remains, and can seem to be at odds
with his role in the community.

Towards the end of Chapter Six, something of the darker
side of the undertaking business is brought into the light
when a very slick corporate organisation moves into Neil's
community. URI have a standardised approach to their business and use the might of their money to pressurise smaller
firms to join them or go out of business. Their sinister, bully-
ing approach brings Neil's father back into his mind, brings
home the realisation that for all his own difficulties with
his father, something in his personality made people in this
place turn to him when they were at their most vulnerable.
Something more than money and cold efficiency made his
father's business work.

In contrast to the time and care Neil's business puts into
the funerals they organise, URI are interested only in profit.
This becomes clear when a woman contacts Neil and Lila in
distress because a local firm of undertakers (now owned by
URI) who said they would bury her son had reneged on their
commitment when they discovered he had died of Aids. When
they go to recover the body they find it lying on the stone
floor of the company's garage in a black body bag with the
word AIDS written across it in red paint. The scene is shocking, reminiscent of the way plague victims were treated in
the Middle Ages, despite the fact that it is happening in the
allegedly more enlightened world of the twentieth century.
Among other things it highlights the fact that encounters
with death remain primal experiences. All the more reason
for those who help us through such encounters to behave
with compassion and decency.

Something else occurs in this chapter which makes the
reader rather uncomfortable. Neil, Lila and Des are ap-

proached by a Mr Samuels to provide three examples of their
coffins for an exhibition he is holding in his art gallery. Even
Neil is initially taken aback to find their coffins being called
'pieces' and seen as artworks. After some momentary hes-
itation, however, they go ahead and contribute a bottle, a
cigarette, and a syringe. The reader is constantly being challenged by the book's black humour, by the use of humour as
a defence mechanism which is assuredly one way with which
undertakers cope with the stress of their work. Readers are
also challenged by the way the creative funeral idea becomes
almost a kind of ghoulish game for the firm throughout Chapters Six and Seven.

Chapter Seven
With Chapter Seven the mood of the novel changes again.
Neil's business comes under more pressure from URI who
bring their 'roadshow' to town to try and interest more local
firms to become part of their operation. Neil and Lila walk
out of the presentation but even this draws sensationalised
press coverage just at a time when Neil seems to be with-
drawing slightly from the initial excitement of the creative
side of their business, becoming more interested in the people than the coffins. He is beginning to feel more. Learning
empathy.

However, clients themselves approach him with odd ideas,
like the Spitfire coffin dropped from another aircraft into the
sea, a coffin in the shape of *Star Trek*'s Starship Enterprise,
even virtual funerals on the internet. For all his active par-
ticipation in all of this, for all his helping people to hold funerals that celebrate the interests of the deceased, there is
almost a sense of things having gone too far too soon. Neil
himself begins to find it hard to keep up with the expecta-
tions he has aroused. For all his involvement in the funeral
business he has still not really answered his question: 'What
happens when you die?' In some way it seems that the nature of his involvement has moved him even further away
from the possibility of an answer.

He is brought up sharp when the same Mr Samuels who
had commissioned the pieces for the art exhibition contacts

him again. When he visits him he finds Samuels in a bright, high-ceilinged room, with the sun streaming in through its bay windows:

> An old comfortable sofa had been pulled across in front of them, and stretched out on it, propped up on cushions, covered by a Mexican blanket, lay Samuels. Sam. And my own breath caught, a sharp gasp at the sight of him. Emaciated, wasted, burned out. (p.262)

Samuels explains that he has been HIV positive for some time and that he now has 'full blown aids' and will be going into a hospice to die very soon. He asks Neil to organise his funeral. He does so, but the shock of Samuels' deterioration hits him hard:

> I couldn't believe the speed of his deterioration, just in a matter of weeks. Even thinner than he'd been, Belsen thin, stark caricature of himself. The nurses told me he'd fallen the day before, his legs had just buckled under him. He was losing the sight in his right eye, damage to the optic nerve. (p.264)

This physical disintegration affects Neil deeply because this time he is involved before the moment of death itself. He is having to observe the process rather than deal with the end product. He finds this hard because he likes Samuels. As he supports Samuels in his last days Samuels also offers support to him. He describes a dream he had and then to make it clear that there was nothing vague or unreal about it adds:

> 'Only that's not what it felt like. Not a dream. It was too vivid. Too real. More real than this.' He looked round the room, then back at me, intense. (p.266)

It is clear that Samuels regards his 'dream' as a powerful and sustaining vision of another reality. In the dream Samuels was by the sea, wanting to dive in, but did not have the strength in his wasted body to do so. A voice invited him in, saying 'It's time', and, as he stepped in, he was transformed:

> 'I had a new body, not flesh, it was made of light. And I woke up in tears, ecstatic. And that's it, I'm ready now. There's no fear. I know I'm more than this.' (p.266)

Perhaps this is the wish-fulfilment dream of a man whose body is racked with pain, a man who is simply tired of trying to get through another day facing the indignity and humiliation of his failing body. It is, however, a moment of complete acceptance, such as those described in many spiritual traditions. The reality of Samuels' vision strikes home to Neil McGraw. It links, too, in the reader's mind with other dreams and visions in the book: the vision in the cellar in Chapter One and the bad acid trip in Chapter Three – as well as echoing back across the years to the narrator's vision of the Virgin Mary in Spence's moving story 'Blue'. The simple message is that we are 'more than this', that we are part of some greater process.

After Samuels' funeral Neil and Lila talk simply about death in a way we have not seen them do before:

> 'It goes so quick,' I said.
>   'What does?'
>   'A life. You can"t grasp it.'
>   'That's the point,' she said. 'If you try to grasp it, you lose it.'
>   'So you have to let go.'
>   'Surrender. Be in the moment.'
>   'Sounds easy.'
>   'Wish it was.'
>   'You batter away at it, year in year out. Then you die.'
> (pp.266–7)

Neil's words recall his father's 'Bottom line. We die' from Chapter One. Lila's words echo William Blake, but also Sri Chinmoy for whom surrender to the love of God, a giving up of our selfish wish to ignore Him, is a crucial concept. For Neil this is a hard lesson. 'No surrender' is the cry he has always heard around him. 'Don't give in.' 'Don't lose face.' Yet Lila's simple words 'Be in the moment' carry a lot of weight. They recall Neil's sense of being completely there in the moment he scattered his father's ashes. They are also about accepting, understanding where we are now. In that understanding there is peace. Neil's wistful 'sounds easy' reminds us just how hard this acceptance is, but, when all else is said and done, that is all there is. That is why Samuels' acceptance of death rings true. He had gone beyond the need to dissemble and had to talk plainly because he knew he would no longer be part of the bright, social world to which he had previously belonged. Even before he died he was living in a different world from the rest of us. The enormity of death makes us think all the more intensely about the sheer wonder of being alive in this world at this very moment.

Chapter Eight
The final chapter in *Way to Go* is short. In it Neil McGraw describes the sudden onset of his own final illness:

> First sign was so slight I almost didn't notice. Thought nothing of it. (p.279)

Like most people, he cannot believe it is happening to him. The difficulty of talking about it, the inability even to think about it is brought home by Rab Deans who has by now taken on Andy's job as driver for the firm:

> Rab came in to visit, was awkward, not knowing where to look. He'd brought me some fruit, in a plastic bag, set it down rustling on the bedside table. Stood there uncomfortable, eventually found the words.
> 'It's a bastard, eh?'
> 'It is that,' I said. 'Hit the coffin-nail right on the head. Death is a bastard.' (p.280)

When Neil receives counselling in hospital he is brought up against the apparent futility of trying to think about death, something sharply expressed once by Hugh MacDiarmid in his poem 'At My Father's Grave':

A livin' man on a deid man thinks
And ony sma'er thocht's impossible.

Neil's counsellor Molly says, 'You're used to dealing with
death', to which Neil answers sharply, 'Not my own.' (p.281)
She talks to him about 'letting go', about acceptance. The conversation echoes the conversation between Neil and Lila after
Samuels' funeral, and reminds us of Samuels' dream. Molly
suggests that Neil try to find a pattern or meaning in his life
by looking on it as a story. He begins to write it down:

> To make this daft life into a story. Write it down, tell it. To
> see it clear, give it shape. To accept it, and let it go. My own
> death the end of it. The answer to my big question on the
> last page. (p. 282)

He explains that he 'wrote it like a novel, changed bits, exag-
gerated for emphasis.' (p.282) Perhaps what he wrote is the
novel we are now reading.

This last chapter is written in shorter sections than the
earlier chapters as if he no longer has the energy to write
much at each sitting. The sections also become increasing-
ly disconnected as if to echo the workings of a mind that is
already moving into another reality, another way of being.
His dead father comes and stands at the end of his bed
and speaks to him in a language he has never heard before and
does not understand, but which makes him wake up crying
(p.283). What is this language of the dead? What message
did his father convey? He does not tell us, but the implication
is that it is the language of love and acceptance. His father's
coming like that echoes Samuels' dream, just as the next section does when Neil talks of an 'intense awareness of light.
Light all around me, flowing through my whole being. Myself
expanding into it, becoming light.' (p.283)

Lila and Des and Neil have a laugh at the death of the grim
minister McNaught who had worked himself up into such a
state while preaching against the ungodly public mourning of
Princess Diana that he had burst into flame where he stood.

Their gloating at this, however, is immediately undercut by the violent nature of Neil's cancer:

> The Reaper came at me in the night, hacked at my bowels again and again with his vicious blade. Said *Make a fucking joke out of this / this / this.* (p.286)

The brutality of the language, the sharp staccato rhythms, make this particularly harrowing.

When he is able to think about his own funeral he chooses:

> A simple pine box, painted sky-blue with that weathered look, a wash, a natural fade. A brush-drawing on the lid in darker blue, a single stroke. A Zen circle, incomplete.
> 'That's all?' said Des.
> 'That's all.' (p.287)

That's all, because Neil has won through to a kind of simplicity, symbolised by the single stroke of the Zen circle. The extremity of his position means he has to think clearly, can no longer allow his mind to be muddied and disturbed by all the 'stuff' we normally think about. The affair is plain and serious and its stark reality has to be faced. As Neil's symptoms worsen and he becomes more and more exhausted, he finds he becomes extremely selective about what he has the energy to read:

> A handful of books. Japanese death verses. Gospel of Ramakrishna. Ray Carver's late poems. A few others. Books that could still speak to me in this last place. (pp.287–8)

Extracts from some of these appear between the chapters of *Way to Go*. One of Carver's poems in particular helps Neil and Lila to cope with thoughts of his coming death. The poem gives an intimate glimpse of Carver's relationship with Tess Gallagher, and was written when they both knew he was dying. It ends:

[...] so. kiss me goodbye now. Here, kiss me again.
Once more. There. That's enough.
Now, my dearest, let me go.
It's time to be on the way. (p.288)

When they have read it they simply hold each other for a long time. In this place words are not enough.

Again his father comes to him 'not speaking in tongues this time'. When he does speak it is with a smile such as Neil has never seen him make before, a smile of compassion and understanding. He says just one thing: *'You have to learn.'* (p.289) Neil is learning, is coming close to the answer he has sought for so long. Another dream or vision of The Reaper reminds us of the old *sadhu* Neil had met at Varanasi. So companionable does the Reaper now seem that Neil feels no fear:

I wanted to ask him my question. I can answer it, he said,
but only in silence. (p.289)

Like all the best answers it cannot be put into words.

The section begins to dissolve into this very silence as Neil passes away:

Fed from a drip. Morphine for the pain. I could go any time.
Next week. Tomorrow. In five minutes. Now. (p.289)

The last few pages describe the funeral Neil had planned. It is not written by him after his death, but is written 'as if he is watching it all' because he knows beforehand how it should unfold. To make this conceit easier for readers to accept Spence reminds them of Tom Sawyer 'at the back of the church, late for his own funeral'. (p.290)

The simple blue coffin is carried in to the music of Bach and, as the mourners settle, the music changes to Laurie Anderson's 'Born, Never Asked', a song that raises pointed questions about the ineffable mystery of human life. To show that he still has faith in his business Neil has Des tell a string of bad jokes because death is 'the ultimate crap joke'. (p.290) The language here is hardly exalted and the whole scene makes for uneasy reading because of our own fixed ideas about what is and is not appropriate on such occasions so that even in death Neil McGraw is challenging us. More fittingly, perhaps, as the coffin slides behind the curtain the voice of Allen Ginsberg is heard singing his moving song, 'Hey Father Death, I'm Flying Home' (p.292).

The last piece of music, however, deliberately circles back to Bach:

> The Bach aria, the *da capo* from the end, back to where we started, complexity resolved in simplicity. Yes we are mortal, the music says, this life ends. But in the moment we can know eternity. (p.293)

Is this the answer to Neil's question? Perhaps, but there can be no proof. Unless of course the description of the funeral is not written looking into the well-planned future, but rather as a present tense account from one who has gone beyond. The book ends with Lila recovering Neil's ashes, putting them into some fireworks, a dozen rockets, so that his remains can be fired into the immensity of the night sky:

> She bends to the first rocket, holds the flame to the touch paper, steps back. It splutters and fizzles, then it catches, flares, swishes into the air trailing smoke. They all cheer and laugh as it explodes, showers sparks. And they take turns, light all the rockets in quick succession, watch them soar, one after another, starburst of colour, momentary mandala, these ashes the last of me scattered into the night. (p. 293)

As the ashes scatter, the dissolution of Neil's body is complete and his voice is heard no more. The rest is silence.

Except for a lovely wee surprise when the reader turns over the last page.

Style and Characterisation

Way To Go is a novel that seems to follow a structure and style that is close to the fable in that it presents a character on a journey or quest in search of wisdom or enlightenment.

Fables have a long history in Scottish literature, the most famous examples perhaps being Robert Henryson's *Morall Fabillis* in the fifteenth century. Those versions of Aesop's fables tell their story then draw an explicit moral at the end. Spence's fable is closer to those of Stevenson in that his 'moral' is embedded in the narrative itself and is rarely made explicit because for these writers such explicitness is limiting. As a meditation teacher, Spence knows the value of 'teaching stories' which reveal their many meanings over time, as the mind of the reader turns over in his or her mind, the events and significance of the tale that is told.

In *Way to Go* the fable structure is clear in the way that Neil McGraw, who could be seen to represent our ordinary selfish nature, gradually moves towards some kind of wisdom by coming into contact with a variety of characters who teach him some new thing that is vital to his development. In some chapters this is very obvious. In chapter one he very obviously goes around asking different people the answer to his question, and like a character in a fable, he always asks in the same way so that the very repetition sets up an understanding of the nature of the quest in the reader's mind. Each of the people he asks gives him a partial answer; it is Neil's task as the man on the quest to piece them all together and to add his own insights.

It is possible to see the characters as archetypes and to see that Spence is subtly using motifs from the tradition of fable and folk-tale to give added resonance to a novel that is obviously set in our contemporary world. The hard-hearted father tests Neil's patience and resilience, as does the bully Rab Deans. Having to deal with these two male figures, Neil learns to define himself as a different kind of person. The graceful young girl Padma and, later, his wife Lila use their femininity to teach him to open up emotionally, to become more understanding and less selfish. Abe Morris teaches Neil very specifically, while Andy the firm's driver, and Auld Jock the joiner teach him valuable lessons more obliquely. The point of many of these teaching stories or fables of course is to suggest that what is really important is that the characters in the stories learn the lessons that are there all around us all the time.

Notes

1 Stevenson wrote a series of *Fables* between 1887 and 1888 and then added to them when he was living in Samoa from 1889. They were appended to the volume containing *Dr Jekyll and Mr Hyde* in the *Collected Works* (1894–1898).

4. CONCLUSION

For Alan Spence the act of writing is a way of making readers think about the nature of their own lives. He turns a clear eye on the poverty and deprivation that denies people access to a full and rewarding life and he is sharply critical of the lack of imagination and failure of vision that still blights our society. While on a surface level his books are entertaining and full of a quietly understated humour as he describes the lives of ordinary people living in a world we all recognise as modern Scotland, they also work on a more subtle level to make us see that there is more to life than the obvious. He does not do this by making big statements or large gestures but he does it by drawing attention to all the small things, the fugitive and elusive moments of insight that are part of all of our lives. By exploring the intimate moments of people's lives he shows us that 'ordinary' lives are full of insight and understanding and he helps to articulate this for those who cannot express their understanding for themselves. His writing is thus filled with a passionate and compassionate sense of the dignity of all.

5. CODA

After the sometimes unsettling black comedy of *Way to Go*, Spence changed the mood and produced three collections of haiku: *Seasons of the Heart, Glasgow Zen,* and *Clear Light* . This was a bit of a return to his roots as his first published book was *ah!*, a collection of fifty haiku. Spence has always admired the pared-down quality of the language of the haiku writers, many of whom were adherents of Zen Buddhism. These short poems have the effect of opening the mind of their readers, hence the title *ah!*. which refers to the great Japanese writer Basho's definition of haiku as the 'ah! of things': that contented sound you make when you suddenly realise what something means. As elsewhere in Alan Spence's work humour and insight go together:

> the sound of the rain
> the sound of the rain
> the sound of the rain

His last novel to date is *The Pure Land* (2006) which is a new departure for him. Set in nineteenth century Japan it tells the real-life story of Thomas Glover, a young Scotsman who went there to make his fortune and became involved in the political upheaval that led to the development of modern Japan. Glover's ambition and drive was such that he became one of the founders of the Mitsubishi Company, as well as having time to be one of the possible models for Puccini's great opera, *Madame Butterfly*. Spence's novel is a fusion of fact and fiction which allows him further to develop his exploration of Eastern spirituality, while dealing with a character in many ways completely at odds with it. It is a valuable addition to a strain of Western literature that attempts to understand a culture that is very different from our own. The last section of *The Pure Land*, which could almost stand on its own as the profoundly moving story of a spiritual life, perhaps points us in the direction Spence's fiction might take after this. Almost every word in this section carries a resonance far beyond its literal meaning. Once again Spence has used language of striking simplicity and clarity to open up the reader's mind. It is a stunning achievement.

6. GLOSSARY OF EASTERN PHILOSOPHICAL TERMS

Dharma: the teachings of the Buddha.

Enlightenment: a state of mind in which we are free from illusion.

Karass: a group of people you are destined to meet who will aid your spiritual development.

Karma: the belief that what you do now has a direct effect on what happens to you later.

Kensho: a brief moment of partial enlightenment.

Koan: an 'unanswerable' question asked by a Zen master to push his or her student beyond normal logic.

Mandala: a circular figure with spokes radiating out from a clearly-defined centre. Traditionally seen as a symbol of wholeness.

Mantra: a short phrase that can be repeated silently or chanted out loud to develop a certain state of mind.

Reincarnation: the belief that we can be born again into another lifetime so that we can work towards enlightenment.

Sadhu: a Hindu holy man

Samsara: the world of illusions in which we live.

Satori: a sharp, sudden moment of complete enlightenment.

Sufism : a mystical tradition of Islam.

Void: for Buddhists, everything in the world comes out of a great emptiness. This is a positive term

Yin and Yang: the two opposing forces that Taoists believe give energy to the world.

Zen: a form of Buddhism that uses meditation to create a mind ripe for Enlightenment, which can then happen suddenly and unexpectedly.

7. BIBLIOGRAPHY

Books by Alan Spence

Prose:
Its Colours They Are Fine, Glasgow: Collins, 1977; London: Phoenix House, 1996
The Magic Flute, Edinburgh: Canongate, 1990
Stone Garden & Other Stories, London: Phoenix House, 1995
Way to Go, London: Phoenix House, 1998
The Pure Land, Edinburgh: Canongate, 2006

Drama:
Sailmaker, Edinburgh: Salamander Press, 1982
Space Invaders, Edinburgh: Salamander Press, 1983
Changed Days: Memories of an Edinburgh Community, London: Hodder & Stoughton 1991

Poetry:
ah! 50 haiku, Jamaica, N.Y.: Agni Press, 1975
Glasgow Zen, Glasgow: Print Studio Press, 1981
Seasons of the Heart, Edinburgh: Canongate, 2000
Glasgow Zen, Edinburgh: Canongate, 2002
Clear Light, Edinburgh: Canongate, 2005

Secondary Sources

Deveney, Catherine: 'Reasons of the Heart', *Scotland on Sunday*, 8 September, 2002

Massie, Allan: 'Sense and Sensibility', *The Scotsman*, 27 August, 1977

Murray, Isobel (ed.): *Scottish Writers Talking 2*, East Linton: Tuckwell Press, 2002

Norris, Fiona (ed.): *Writers in Scotland*, London: Hodder & Stoughton, 1994

Royle, Trevor (ed.) *Jock Tamson's Bairns*, London: Hamish Hamilton, 1977 (contains Spence's autobiographical essay 'Boom Baby')

Taylor, Alan: 'Beyond Belief', *The Sunday Herald*, 16 March 2003